Where the Rivers Meet: Jesús Moncada

Five Leaves/Anglo-Catalan Society Occasional Papers include:

Dictionary for the Idle
by Joan Fuster
Translated by Dominic Keown

A Female Scene: three plays by Catalan women
Àngels Aymar, Araceli Bruch and Mercè Sarrias
Translated by Marion Peter Holt, Laura Melcion and John London
Edited by Dr Montserrat Roser i Puig

Trueta
Àngels Aymar
Published in Catalan and English
Translation from the Catalan by Dr Montserrat Roser i Puig

Where the Rivers Meet: Jesús Moncada

Edited by Kathryn Crameri

Five Leaves Publications
in association with the Anglo-Catalan Society
www.fiveleaves.co.uk

Where the Rivers Meet: Jesús Moncada
Edited by Kathryn Crameri

Published in 2011
by Five Leaves Publications,
PO Box 8786, Nottingham NG1 9AW
www.fiveleaves.co.uk

in association with
the Anglo-Catalan Society
www.anglo-catalan.org

Anglo-Catalan Society Occasional Papers
New Series

Collection © Kathryn Crameri,
Five Leaves Publications
and the Anglo-Catalan Society

Copyright for individual essays and
translations rests with the contributors

Cover images © Ajuntament de Mequinensa
and Heirs of Jesús Moncada,
see http://www.jesusmoncada.cat/albums/

ISBN: 978 1 907869 11 2

Five Leaves acknowledges
financial support from
Arts Council England

Five Leaves and the Anglo-Catalan Society
thank the Institute Ramon Llull
for their support for this title

Contents

Preface	7
Introduction (Kathryn Crameri)	9
Literary context and critical reception	12
Chapter 1 Catalan Narrative 1970-2005 (Stewart King)	22
Chapter 2 Jesús Moncada: A Biographical Sketch (Hèctor Moret)	42
Discovery and learning of the written language	45
First texts and literary prizes	46
Històries de la mà esquerra	47
El Cafè de la Granota	48
Camí de sirga	50
La galeria de les estàtues	51
Estremida memòria	52
Calaveres atònites	52
Cabòries estivals i altres proses volanderes	52
General characteristics	53
Chapter 3 The Short Stories: The Universe and Voices of Mequinensa (Sandrine Ribes)	56
Organisation and themes of the three collections of short stories	56
Moncada's universe	61
The characters	66
The voice of the people	77
'Old Sheet Music', translated by Judith Willis	94
Chapter 4 The Novels: Myth, History, Storytelling and Memory (Kathryn Crameri)	105

Camí de sirga (1988)	107
La galeria de les estàtues (1992)	110
Estremida memòria	114
Themes: Myth, History, Memory and Storytelling	117
Local, national and global histories	123
Genre and literary influences	128

Extract from *Estremida memòria*, 134
translated by Kathryn Crameri

Select Bibliography 147

Contributors and translators 161

Preface

This volume is the result of a collaboration between four scholars working in different countries and languages. The editor, Kathryn Crameri, works at the University of Sydney, Australia, and has had an interest in the works of Jesús Moncada since stumbling across a translation of his first novel in a university library in the mid-1990s. Stewart King, also Australian, works at Monash University and is an expert in contemporary Catalan and Spanish fiction. Hèctor Moret, on the other hand, is a fellow countryman of Moncada and a personal friend of the late author as well as having made important contributions to the study of his work. Finally, Sandrine Ribes works at the University Montpellier III, Paul Valéry, and chose the work of Jesús Moncada as the subject of the doctoral thesis she completed in 2006. This international collaboration is a reflection of the goals and motivation for this volume: to bring Moncada's work to the attention of a wider audience outside his homeland, where he is very highly regarded.

All quotations from Catalan, French and Spanish have been translated into English for the convenience of the reader. All translations are by Kathryn Crameri unless otherwise stated. Titles of novels and short stories are only translated the first time they appear. The bibliography is a selection of the most useful sources and is based on a list provided by Hèctor Moret, supplemented by information from the comprehensive bibliography compiled by Sandrine Ribes for her doctoral thesis.

The following abbreviations are used in the endnotes to refer to the works of Jesús Moncada:

HME   *Històries de la mà esquerra*
CDG   *El Cafè de la Granota*
CA   *Calaveres atònites*
CdS   *Camí de sirga*
GE   *La galeria de les estàtues*
EM   *Estremida memòria*

The authors would like to thank the Anglo-Catalan Society for its support in publishing this volume, and Edicions 62 for giving us permission to include the translations of Moncada's work. We are also very grateful to Judith Willis for contributing the translation of *D'uns vells papers de música*.

Introduction
Kathryn Crameri

Jesús Moncada (1941-2005) was one of the key figures in Catalan literature at the end of the twentieth century, as is clear from the reception of his work both by the public and the majority of critics. His writing has been translated into over twenty languages and won several important literary prizes, including the *Premi Ciutat de Barcelona, Premi Nacional de la Crítica,* and the *Premi de les Lletres Aragoneses.* In 2001 he received the highest honour that can be given by the Catalan Autonomous Government (the *Generalitat de Catalunya):* the Cross of Saint George *(Creu de Sant Jordi).* Despite this high level of recognition of his work, his publications are few in number, since he started to publish relatively late and was not a prolific writer. His death at a the age of only 64 was sadly another factor in this small number of works of fiction, which is mainly made up of three collections of short stories and three novels.

Moncada was born and brought up in a small town in Aragón at the border of Catalonia in an area known as La Franja. This is why his first language was Catalan rather than Spanish, since La Franja sits in a transitional area between the two languages. The town itself — Mequinensa (Mequinenza in Spanish) — has become forever associated with Moncada's work since it forms the backdrop for the vast majority of his fiction. The town could also be described as the main force behind Moncada's literary creativity. His experience of growing up there, by the river Ebro with its mines, barges and particular social mix, marks his language, his sense of place and time, and his observations of humanity. Importantly, historical events associated with the town also provided him with a framework on which to pin much of his fiction. One particularly vital event was its destruction in 1971 during the construction of the Riba-Roja dam, which became the subject of his first and best-known novel, *Camí de sirga* (*The Towpath*, 1988).

This event also had an influence on Moncada's other form of expression, his painting. Before putting aside art to concentrate on literature at the beginning of the 1980s, his work had been the subject of a number of exhibitions both in Mequinensa and around Barcelona. Many of his paintings represented the daily life of men and women in Mequinensa, but portrayed them with hollow faces or torsos, as if the soul and identity of the people had been torn out of them by the impending destruction of the town. As Mercè Ibarz puts it, the figures he painted 'obtenen una gran expressivitat de desconcert, submissió, preocupació, incertesa' ('show a great expressiveness, of unease, submission, worry, uncertainty'). 'La buidor dels cossos sense res a dins seu' is framed by everyday objects that appear to have been frozen in time: 'cafès que cauen, licors en suspensió, cartes, sabates i altres petits objectes en un moviment lliure i sense gravetat, dispersos i perduts per un espai volàtil' ('the emptiness of the bodies with nothing inside', [...] 'spilt cups of coffee, liquids in suspension, cards, shoes and other small objects in free fall but without gravity, dispersed and lost in a volatile space').[1] It is clear that Moncada was inescapably marked by the fate of his community and it is no wonder that the people of Mequinensa are fiercely proud of his attempts to save, through literature, some of what the town meant to its inhabitants.

Despite this very local focus, Moncada's work has consistently been praised for its universal appeal, which is one of the reasons for the literary prizes that it won. It also explains the numerous translations either of his novels or short stories that have been carried out in a wide variety of languages: Spanish, German, English, Italian, Swedish, Hebrew, Polish, Japanese and Vietnamese to name just a few. The most translated novel is *Camí de sirga;* in fact this is the only one that has been translated into English (poor sales — possibly due to a lack of marketing — meant that translations of the other two novels have not been commissioned). In contrast, the second novel (*La galeria de les estàtues* — The Statue Gallery) has been translated into German, and the third (*Estremida memòria* - Jolted Memory) is available in French. Interest in both translating and studying Moncada's work has, however, continued since his death, and several collections of essays have also been published in Catalonia and Aragón in homage to the author.

Importantly, Moncada's work is often taught in Catalan and Aragonese schools, where the short stories especially have become important resources for both literary and linguistic activities. This has resulted in the publication of a number of 'Reading Guides' (*Guies de lectura*) to help teachers and students get the most out the works, and *El Cafè de la Granota* (The Frog Café) is available in an educational edition with notes and suggested activities by Hèctor Moret. These are complemented by a growing amount of information available on Moncada on the internet, which includes a comprehensive guide to Mequinensa and its surroundings, linking real places with Moncada's fictional representation of them ('Espais literaris de Jesús Moncada', www.jesusmoncada.cat).

Despite the popularity of Moncada's writing, the body of critical work on both the novels and short stories is somewhat patchy, although it is growing steadily. The majority of publications consist of reviews, interviews, brief notes in newspapers and *guies de lectura*. There are fewer in-depth studies of Moncada's work, and very little has been published in English, although there are encouraging signs such as the fact that a number of PhD theses on Moncada are now underway both in Catalonia and elsewhere. (Sandrine Ribes was, as far as we know, the first person to complete a thesis on Moncada.) This introductory volume is partly designed to make up for the lack of critical work in English and we hope that it will also stimulate further research and translation. However, its main aim is simply to introduce readers to the rich rewards of reading the work of Jesús Moncada.

This introduction continues by looking at the literary influences that shaped Moncada's writing, the critical reception of his work, and the main themes that have drawn the critics' attention. In the next chapter, Stewart King provides an overview of Catalan literary production during the period in which Moncada was active as a writer. This is followed by an intellectual biography of Moncada and a brief introduction to each of his published works, by Hèctor Moret. Chapter 3 is an investigation of the short stories by Sandrine Ribes, while chapter 4, by Kathryn Crameri, tackles the novels. Each of these is followed by an example of Moncada's work in English translation: the short story *D'uns vells papers de música*, translated by Judith Willis, and a fragment of *Estremida memòria*, translated by Kathryn Crameri. Finally we include a select bibliography of works by and about Jesús Moncada.

Literary context and critical reception

In terms of the literary influences we might see in Moncada's writing, it is clear that these come from a broad range of Catalan, Spanish and foreign literature. When asked in an interview what he read during his formative years, Moncada gave a long list of authors or particular works, among which were *Mirall trencat* by Mercè Rodoreda, *Bearn* by Llorenç Villalonga, *Les històries naturals* by Joan Perucho and the short stories of Pere Calders.[2] Spanish and Latin American authors mentioned included Baroja, Valle-Inclán, Fuentes, Rulfo and Carpentier. However, he stated that his main interest at that time was Italian literature — Levi, Pratolini and Pavese, among others — and also mentioned Chekov and Kazandzakis. His later work as a translator continued this exposure to other literatures, and he was said to be an avid reader. Nevertheless, he rejected the idea that his own work could be unproblematically placed within a certain literary tradition. In an interview in 1971 he stated that 'Los moldes en literatura molestan mucho. Muchísimo. Anulan la personalidad del escritor. Escribo a mi manera' ('literary moulds are a nuisance, a real nuisance. They negate the personality of the writer. I write in my own way').[3] This may be one reason why there was a perception among some critics that his writing was somewhat out of step with the main development of Catalan literature during the 1970s and 80s.

There are several reasons for situating Moncada outside the mainstream of Catalan literature despite being one of its most successful exponents. Firstly, the fact that he started to publish relatively late in life meant that he was rather separated from other Catalan writers born in the 1940s such as Terenci Moix, Montserrat Roig and Biel Mesquida. Even authors born several years later, such as Quim Monzó (b. 1952), had already started publishing significant works before Moncada. These writers came to be identified as the *Generació dels 70,* since this is when their first 'mature' works were published and they were regarded as having several features in common. These include having lived through the post-war period and experienced its hardships, but also having been part of the tourist boom and *apertura* of the 1960s, not to mention having their cultural experiences shaped by new media such as television and Hollywood movies.[4] This led them to adopt generally experimental styles of writing in order to overcome the perceived stagnation of the Catalan novel of that period, and to find new modes of expression for the different realities they faced. It is in this aspect that Moncada is thought to differ from his contemporaries, since although many of the linking factors apply to him too, it is his choice of style and subject matter that sets him apart. Moncada himself said that 'si bé em vinculo històricament a la generació, perquè evidentment no sóc un escriptor que hagi nascut per generació espontània, no m'hi sento lligat literàriament' ('even though I do have a historical connection to the generation, since obviously I'm not a writer that appeared *sui generis*, I don't feel any literary connection with it').[5]

This means that rather than grouping Moncada within the *Generació dels 70*, to which his birth date might suggest that he belonged, he has tended to be classified under a different heading, as a writer of 'rural literature'. Obviously this refers to the fact that the majority of his novels and stories are set in Mequinensa rather than in the city, but this rather simple tag hides quite a complex commentary on Moncada's place in Catalan literature. Rather than being purely descriptive it also implies a value judgement, to the extent that many critics were worried that it was not good for Catalan literature that its major successes were 'rural' and 'nostalgic' rather than 'urban' and 'modern'.[6] Josep M. Lluró, for example, described the rural novel in 1992 as 'un fenomen sobredimensionat, estèticament sobrevalorat' ('a phenomenon that has been blown out of proportion and aesthetically overvalued').[7] His criticism is based on the fact that the rural novel does not challenge the reader or search for new literary possibilities. Instead, he claims, it simply 'reconstructs' a lost world from a nostalgic and essentialist point of view that demands no intellectual effort from the reader.[8]

According to Isidor Cònsul, most of the writers producing 'rural literature' can be classified as such because they either prefer a rural setting for its symbolism or need to create an entire mythical geography as the basis for their narrative.[9] Memory, nostalgia and the evocation of the landscape are key elements for those who create mythical geographies, some of whom — according to Cònsul — are basically producing 'elegies per un món perdut' ('elegies to a lost world'). Interestingly, he raises Moncada's work (or at least *Camí de sirga*) above others in this category because of its 'tarannà vital i jocund que més aviat l'allunya del plor i del plany elegíac' ('lively and joyful character, which actually distances it from sorrow or elegiac lament'). However, Moncada does not escape Cònsul's main point, which is that Catalan literature should get the rural novel out of its system and turn towards urban modernity instead.

One of the other novelists who tends to be classified under the 'rural' heading is Maria Barbal, the author of successful novels such as *Pedra de tartera* (1985) and *Carrer Bolívia* (1999).

Like Moncada, she first came to the public's attention in the 1980s. Both authors have been critical of the obsession with pigeonholing their work and the rejection of 'rurality'. Maria Barbal puts this down to the 'desig català de cosmopolitisme a qualsevol preu' which explains 'l'instint destructor contra obres que puguin entranyar dubtes en relació a la modernitat' ('Catalan desire for cosmopolitanism at any price'; 'the destructive instinct regarding works that might give rise to doubts about modernity').[10] When asked in a recent interview whether she had herself deliberately moved from 'rural' to 'urban' themes in order to avoid the stigma of being considered a rural novelist, Maria Barbal replied 'No escric per aconseguir cap títol ni per negar etiquetes que, en definitiva, ha posat algú en un moment determinat i que després han quedat una mica somortes' ('I don't write in order to come under a particular heading, nor to react against labels that, in fact, someone has used at a particular moment in time and that have since become a bit jaded').[11] Moncada had a similar view, and recalled joking with Quim Monzó about the inaccuracy of the label.[12] Furthermore, Moncada rejected the idea that Mequinensa could be unambiguously described as a rural setting, since much of the town's identity and economic activity centred around mining and transport. As far as Moncada was concerned, the debate on 'rural versus urban' was 'una polèmica que no anava enlloc' ('a controversy that got us nowhere').[13]

He was similarly unimpressed by attempts to link him to magic realism. This tendency was mainly found in critics who saw the literary Mequinensa Moncada had created as a reworking of Gabriel García Márquez's Macondo, although it was also a response to some of the episodes in Moncada's work that might be seen as verging on the fantastic. Moncada himself rejected the comparison on both counts, stating that he had no particular interest in Latin American literature of the 1960s when magic realism was all the rage, and had certainly not set out to create a new Macondo. Furthermore, 'Els episodis que poden semblar més "màgics" de *Camí de sirga*, per exemple, són reals, comprovables' ('the episodes that might seen most "magical" in *Camí de sirga,* for example, are real, verifiable.').[14] If there is any literary influence to be thanked for his skill in this area, he states, it is Pere Calders who should receive the credit.

One of the other (more individual) ways in which Moncada's work was marked out in the eyes of the critics was to do with his use of language. Many of the critical studies that have been published look specifically at this aspect, and in some detail. Several aspects of Moncada's style are of obvious interest, including his use of localisms, the richness of his vocabulary, and his gift for the ironic turn of phrase. These make his work relatively challenging for a non-native speaker of Catalan, who may encounter expressions that are not easily understood even with the aid of a good dictionary. This complexity of style and lexis is one of the features of Moncada's work that has contributed to singling him out as one of the great Catalan writers of the twentieth century.

One of the aspects of his use of language that has been investigated by people such as Mercè Biosca, Hèctor Moret, Sandrine Ribes and Judith Willis is his choice of names: either of places, boats or people. For example, Judith Willis (in the first article on his work published in English) commented that the richness and inventiveness of names in *Camí de sirga* was a challenge for her as a translator. Proper names such as Senyor Jaume de Torres or Aleix de Segarra, for example, 'have a weight and a texture to them — a key concept in the novel — and their function goes beyond that of mere identification onto another plane, almost organic'.[15] Moncada himself said he used a mixture of real and invented names, whether for people (including nicknames), places or boats. His main concern in naming people was to make sure that, in a novel with so many characters, each of them was readily identifiable to the reader so that there was no confusion.[16] Mercè Biosca also notes his obvious delight in creating names, which are sometimes humorous or ironic.[17] However, she stresses that it is normally only nicknames that directly reflect the characteristics of the people to whom they have been assigned. Having examined the meanings of the names used in *La galeria de les estàtues* she concludes that many of the characters' first names bear no relation to their personality or role in the novel. Their given names are therefore randomly assigned, as they would be in real life, which indicates that Moncada was not trying to create symbolic characters by giving them first names that the reader is supposed to find significant.[18]

Other aspects of language that have aroused interest include the use of 'localisms', (linguistic features specific to the variety of Catalan spoken in the *Franja d'Aragó*), and the incorporation of features associated with oral language, especially in dialogue, monologues, and when the narration comes from the point of view of a particular character. Mercè Biosca has carried out a number of very thorough studies of Moncada's use of phrases, refrains and localisms (see bibliography). Interestingly, he quite often modified them or used expressions that cannot be found in lexicographical publications, which meant that Biosca often had to resort to asking him personally where the phrase had come from. She has now prepared a database of such expressions in his work, which will be especially valuable to translators who are having trouble understanding them or finding equivalents in their own language. Nevertheless, as will be seen in the chapters that follow this introduction, the basis of Moncada's literary language was standard Catalan. Non-standard elements are used judiciously and sparingly, in order to create an impression of dialectal features in the language of the people of Mequinensa rather than faithfully recreating their variety of Catalan. This also contributes to what Hèctor Moret describes as 'a tone of oral language that make them seem as if the tales had been gathered directly from the voice of the townspeople'.[19] Sandrine Ribes' chapter on Moncada's short stories in this volume will explore this idea of 'orality' in depth.

Other than language, the main aspects of Moncada's work that have drawn critics' attention have been his literary explorations of myth, memory, storytelling and history. For example, both Kathryn Crameri and Sandrine Ribes have published articles on the use of myth in *Camí de sirga* in which they stress the complex ties Moncada weaves between myth and history. Whereas some critics have seen his use of myth as facile,[20] both Ribes and Crameri argue that there is more to it than simply turning the real Mequinensa into a literary myth. Moncada also draws on parallels between the historical fate of Mequinensa and the 'fall and flood' category of myths, including the biblical myths of Noah and the expulsion of Adam and Eve from the Garden of Eden. Sandrine Ribes has also identified other mythical elements that are connected to the symbolism of the river, and to the rituals carried out by the people whose lives depend on it.[21] Furthermore, Moncada in all his fiction reveals how his literary Mequinensa creates its own myths of itself in order to form a collective history that helps the community survive and prosper. This means that the themes of myth and history are intimately connected to those of collective memory and storytelling. This will be explored in greater detail in chapter 4.

This intimate history of the community is framed by carefully-chosen references to historical events, which are more than just a backdrop. In all three of his novels, Moncada links the fate of Mequinensa very closely to the broader history of the country in which it is situated. He also takes the opportunity to make ironic comments or direct criticism of key figures or events, especially of course the Franco regime. The care with which he incorporates verifiable historical information has apparently caused some of his readers to assume that this means that much of what he writes has a historical truth behind it. Moncada was very clear on this point, writing in a note at the start of *Camí de sirga* for example, that the book was not a history of the events surrounding Mequinensa's destruction. Nevertheless, he commented in an interview that 'yo no soy ni un historiador ni un cronista, pero en mi creación literaria hay mucho de crónica y una base histórica cierta y además expurgada, pero no con mentalidad de historiador sino de novelista. Esta precisión a veces incluso tengo que hacérsela a los mequinenzanos para que no confundan la creación literaria con la historia' ('I am not a historian or chronicler, but my literary creation often acts as a chronicle and has a real, select historical basis, not from the point of view of a historian but a novelist. Sometimes I even have to remind the people of Mequinensa about this so that they don't confuse literature with history').[22] Nevertheless, Moncada's work could be said to exist in a space between fiction and history.[23]

Moncada's use of humour and irony, another of the distinctive features of his work, is intimately connected to his sense of the relationship between ordinary people and the historical events that touch them. Many of the characters he creates are viewed through a humorous or ironic lens. In the case of sympathetic characters, this humour is gentle and even loving, whereas others are treated with biting irony. In this case, the character treated in this way is often someone who is being used as a representative of an institution or who wields some kind of authority.[24] In this way, Moncada satirises certain aspects of Spanish history, especially the Franco regime. On the other hand, the human failings of ordinary people are gently ridiculed but ultimately pardoned. In fact, it is significant when the protagonists are exempted from this humour. For example, Dalmau of *La galeria de les estàtues* receives neither humorous nor ironic treatment, which indicates that his role is essentially tragic. The same is true of the main characters in *Estremida memòria*, and for the same reason.

The two extracts from Moncada's work that we have chosen to translate for this volume certainly illustrate Moncada's ability to create very human characters, and the humour that gives them depth even when the theme of the work is very serious. As translations, they can only hint at his craftsmanship with the Catalan language. Nevertheless they provide a good illustration of the aspects of Moncada's writing that have captivated readers and critics alike.

Notes

[1] Mercè Ibarz, 'Apreciacions sobre un univers pictòric', *Urc* 21, 2006, 99-103, p. 100.

[2] Josep M. Muñoz, 'Jesús Moncada: la memòria d'un món negat', first published in *L'Avenç* (1/2/2004), reproduced in *Jesús Moncada. Su universo literario* ed. by Ramón Acín (Gobierno de Aragón, 2005), p. 55.

[3] Xavier Moret, *Retrats: Jesús Moncada* (Barcelona: Associació d'Escriptors en Llengua Catalana, 2005), p. 25.

[4] Guillem-Jordi Graells and Oriol Pi de Cabanyes, *La generació literària dels 70* (Barcelona: Pòrtic, 1971), p. 11.

[5] Marta Nadal, *Vint escriptors catalans* (Barcelona: Publicacions de l'Abadia de Montserrat, 1997), p. 190.

[6] X. Moret, p. 37.

[7] Josep M. Lluró, 'Tendències de la narrativa catalana dels vuitanta', in *70-80-90 Literatura (Dues dècades des de la tercera i última)*, ed. by Àlex Broch et al. (Valencia: Quaderns 3 i 4, 1992), 113-39, p. 129.

[8] Lluró, pp. 129-35.

[9] Isidor Cònsul, 'Geografies mítiques', *Lletra de canvi* 31-32, 1990, 8-12, pp. 9, 10, 12.

[10] Maria Barbal, 'Coses de la vida', *Urc 21*, 2006, 36-9, p. 37.

[11] Interview with Maria Barbal in *El País* 31/5/08 by Costa-Pau.

[12] 'Yo soy subjetivo, claro, pero pienso que es difícil dar a mi obra la etiqueta de rural. El ambiente mequinenzano no es precisamente rural. Es más bien industrial, donde el proletariado tiene una gran importancia desde finales del XIX... Estas etiquetas que, además, pretenden valorar una obra son un disparate. Una obra es buena o mala independientemente de si se desarrolla en Mequinenza o en el paseo de Gràcia. Al lector sueco o alemán o japonés que yo sea de Mequinenza le importa poco, si es que sabe dónde está Mequinenza. Quim Monzó y yo nos tomamos a broma estos temas y cuando coincidimos en algún lugar intercambiamos etiquetas y él me dice: "Hola, urbano"; y yo le digo: "Hola, rural".' From an interview with Antón Castro available on http://purnasenozierzo.blogia.com/2005/junio.php (accessed 6/6/08).

[13] 'Jesús Moncada, de Mequinensa a Torrelloba', *El País,* 13 February 1992 ('Quadern'). Cited in X. Moret, p. 38.

[14] X. Moret, p. 36.

[15] Judith Willis, 'Proper Names in Camí de sirga by Jesús Moncada', *Donaire,* 8 (June 1997), 74-8, p. 74.
[16] Sandrine Ribes, 'L'Oeuvre de Jesús Moncada: Quand l'écriture devient mémoire', unpublished PhD thesis, Université Montpellier III — Paul Valéry, 2006, p. 494.
[17] Mercè Biosca, 'Noms de casa, renoms i zoònims en l'obra de Jesús Moncada', *Actes del XIVè Col·loqui de la Societat d'Onomàstica.* Publicacions de la Universitat d'Alacant, 1(1991), 269-77.
[18] Mercè Biosca, L'onomàstica en *La galleria de les estàtues'*, in *Actes del XIXè Col·loqui General de la Societat d'Onomàstica (Butlletí interior de la Societat d'Onomàstica,* 55, 1996, Institut d'Estudis del Baix Cinca, Calaceit, 65-78.
[19] See the end of chapter 2 of this volume.
[20] Lluró, pp. 132-5.
[21] Sandrine Ribes, 'Le mythe dans *Camí de sirga* de Jesús Moncada', *Revue d'Études Catalanes,* 2, 1999, 159-181, pp. 172-80.
[22] Antón Castro, interview with Jesús Moncada, http://antoncastro.blogia.com/2007/072802-jesus-moncada-otra-entrevista-.php, accessed October 2008.
[23] Ribes, 'L'œuvre', pp. 210-15 & 217.
[24] Ribes, 'L'œuvre', pp. 237-50.

Chapter 1

Catalan Narrative 1970-2005
Stewart King

While it is true that political factors can shape literary production, it is particularly relevant for twentieth-century Catalonia in which two specific events have had an enormous influence on Catalan writing. The first was the victory of the rebel forces led by Francisco Franco against the democratically-elected Popular Front government of Spain in the Spanish Civil War (1936-39). This brutal war in which approximately half a million Spaniards died and a further million were forced into exile was as much a struggle over different conceptions of Spain and Spanishness as it was over issues of democracy and fascism, social justice and the maintenance of traditional social relations.[1] For Catalonia, which supported the Popular Front government, Franco's victory was disastrous, as it allowed the dictator to enforce a series of prohibitive laws against the so-called separatist tendencies that Franco believed threatened Spain's national unity. As a result, following the occupation of Catalonia by National forces, speaking Catalan publicly was proscribed and those caught often suffered beatings or arrest. The teaching of Catalan in schools was also banned, and Catalan studies at university were abolished. Furthermore, in the early days of the regime, publishing in Catalan was prohibited and, in scenes reminiscent of Nazi Germany, Catalan-language books were thrown onto bonfires or pulped.[2] However, from the mid-1940s (shortly after Jesús Moncada was born) the regime did relax slightly the restrictions on the use of Catalan, and books slowly began appearing in Catalan, some in clandestine editions. Although many Catalans continued to use

Catalan during the dictatorship, the effects of the Francoist cultural and linguistic policies cannot be underestimated. Combined with the arrival of large numbers of impoverished Castilian-speaking migrants to Catalonia, these policies meant that by the time of Franco's death in 1975 approximately only 50 percent of the population spoke Catalan and even fewer could read it.[3]

The restoration of democracy following the dictator's death was the second event to shape the growth of Catalan writing. In the new Spanish constitution of 1978, Spain's cultural and linguistic diversity was celebrated, rather than pilloried. In those regions where languages other than Castilian were spoken, these attained co-official status, and limited political and administrative responsibilities were devolved initially to the three so-called 'historical nationalities' — the Basque Country, Catalonia and Galicia — and later to 14 other autonomous communities. In Catalonia, the regional government — the Generalitat — was provisionally established in 1977 and, following its formal recognition, the first elections were held in 1980.

The Generalitat moved quickly to restore Catalan — long the cornerstone of Catalan identity — to its place as the principal language of daily communication in Catalonia. The buzz word for this process was 'normalització' (normalisation), which, although initially associated with linguistic policy, came to represent an attempt to 'transformar Catalunya en una societat *normal*, és a dir, una societat en què la llengua pròpia de Catalunya esdevingui hegemònica, en què tota la ciutadania comparteixi un sentit d'identitat nacional catalana i basat en les tradicions culturals del país, i en què les infraestructures culturals, els hàbits de consum cultural i l'equilibri entre alta cultura i cultura de masses siguin comparables als de qualsevol altra societat europea avançada' ('transform Catalonia into a *normal* society. That is, in a society in which Catalonia's own language would be hegemonic, in which all citizens would share a sense of Catalan national identity based on the country's cultural traditions, and in which the cultural infrastructure, the consumption of culture and the balance between high and mass culture are comparable to those of any other advanced European society').[4]

To this end, the Generalitat reintroduced in 1978 the teaching of Catalan at all levels of schooling. In 1976 *Avui* — the first Catalan-language daily newspaper since 1939 — was launched, and in 1983 TV3 — the Catalan equivalent of the BBC — began broadcasting on television and radio. The introduction of television and radio was an important step in the development of light, mass culture, which was, in particular, seen as crucial to the normalisation process.[5] Indeed, the first dubbed episode of the American 1980s soap opera *Dallas* has become a mythical moment in Catalan modern folklore.

Contemporaneous with the expansion of the local mass-media industry, a boom in Catalan-language publishing took place. Whereas in 1975 only 611 books were published in Catalan (3.4 percent of the total number of books published in Spain), by 1990 this had risen to 4,838 (11.4 percent of the Spanish market). In 2001, this number had again increased to 9,045 titles.[6] This boom was made possible by generous public subsidies as well as the introduction of numerous literary prizes offered by cultural organisations, publishing houses, and local and regional governments which aimed to encourage Catalans to write in Catalan.

The issue of literary prizes in Catalonia, however, has been the source of much soul-searching, as a perennial debate about quantity over quality has been played out in the pages of newspapers, cultural magazines and in various academic fora. While the question of literary quality is obviously subjective and therefore problematic, the term is at the centre of a debate about the state of post-Franco Catalan literature and its institutional support. In particular, many cultural figures have questioned the need for so many different literary prizes (1,249 prizes in total in 2000-2001).[8] The founder of the *La Magrana* publishing house, Carles-Jordi Guardiola, for example, has argued that there are too many prizes for a country like Catalonia, given that 'un país com el nostre no té capacitat per a produir massa novel·les bones a l'any' ('a country like ours does not have the capacity to produce that many good novels each year').[8] Furthermore, Josep-Anton Fernàndez argues that if prizes are supposed to be an indication of quality, then the sheer number of prizes actually serves to undermine this objective, as quality cannot be assured and readers can no longer trust that winning a specific prize, even the significant prizes, such as the Sant Jordi or Ramon Llull prizes, is a guarantor of good literature.[9]

This support for the media and publishing industries has resulted in a major shift in Catalan cultural production, as in a relatively short period of time Catalan culture has gone from being actively persecuted to being recognised and even, to a certain extent, institutionalised. This shift, however, has led to an impression that under the dictatorship Catalan writers suffered, but nevertheless produced great works of literature, whereas literature produced during the democratic period has involved less suffering, but is of a poorer standard. While this is to some extent true, there are nonetheless many Catalan-language writers who have produced excellent novels and short stories since the restoration of democracy to Spain.

Although dates and events — such as the death of Franco — can serve as convenient shorthand for change, a shift in Catalan literature was already observable before the dictator's demise. Indeed, as early as 1971 Guillem-Jordi Graells and Oriol Pi de Cabanyes identified the existence of a new generation in their *La generació literària dels 70,* a collection of interviews with young writers born — like Moncada — in the 1940s. Although the validity of identifying generations has been questioned, critics note that writers, including Terenci Moix, Montserrat

Roig, Quim Monzó, Biel Mesquida, Pere Gimferrer and Oriol Pi de Cabanyes, do all share a range of experiences which have shaped their literary production. These experiences include the post-war repression of Catalan culture which meant that they were largely autodidacts in Catalan culture, the Cold War and Spain's transformation from an isolated, traditional society to an advanced capitalist one. Furthermore, these writers incorporated into Catalan literature American pop culture, particularly music, comics and cinema, as well as kitsch aesthetics, on which they were raised.[10]

According to Àlex Broch, these writers can be divided into two main camps: the reformers and the transgressors.[11] The first group set out to renew realist literature, telling stories in more interesting ways. Montserrat Roig's *L'òpera quotidiana* (The Everyday Opera, 1982) is an example of this, as this polyphonic novel takes the form of an opera with different characters either alone or together performing 'duets, cavatines, recitatius and arias', (duets, cavatinas [a short solo song resembling a simple aria], recitatives [the narrative parts of an oratorio with or without accompanying voices] and arias). Although not a member of the 'seventies generation', Mercè Rodoreda's later fiction is also an example of this. Arguably the most important Catalan novelist of the twentieth century, Rodoreda was born in 1909, forced into exile at the end of the Civil War and only returned to Catalonia in the mid-1970s. Her most famous work is *La plaça del Diamant* (*The Time of the Doves*, 1962), a darkly realistic novel about a young, working-class woman in Barcelona from the 1920s until after the war. Rodoreda's return to Catalonia, however, marked a shift in her fiction with *Mirall trencat* (*A Broken Mirror*, 1974), a narrative which is divided into over 50 short chapters, each of which — like the shards of the broken mirror of the title — offers a slightly different perspective.

Perhaps the best known of the realist writers, Baltasar Porcel was one of the most internationally acclaimed writers from

Catalonia and, indeed, before his death in 2009 he was the Principality's great hope for the Nobel Prize for Literature. Porcel eschews avant-garde or experimental writing, arguing that it 'goes no further than an ingeniousness and exhibitionism that seeks to find expression by means of distortion'.[12] Instead, his best novels, including *Difunts sota els ametllers en flor* (The Deceased that Lie under Almond Trees in Bloom, 1970), *Cavalls cap a la fosca* (*Horses into the Night*, 1975) and *Les primaveres i les tardors* (*Springs and Autumns*, 1986), recreate a mythical community based on the Mallorcan town, Andratx, where Porcel was born. Central to these works is the importance of memory in shaping the collective experience of this mythical community. For this reason, Porcel — like Moncada — is often compared to the Latin American magical realist writers, in particular Gabriel García Márquez.

The group of writers who made up the transgressors, including Terenci Moix, Pere Gimferrer, Biel Mesquida, Oriol Pi de Cabanyes and Quim Monzó (in his early novels), rejected narrative realism in favour of anti-novels in the French *nouveau roman* tradition which sought to destroy the centrality of plot and character. The Mallorcan writer, Biel Mesquida's *L'adolescent de sal* (The Adolescent of Salt, 1975) is perhaps the most (in)famous example of this, as it combines newspaper clippings, graffiti, film scripts, diary entries, and other genres in a complex narrative structure.[13] Oriol Pi de Cabanyes, a university lecturer and essayist, as well as novelist and short story writer, won the Prudenci Bertrana prize in 1973 for *Oferiu flors als rebels que fracassaren* (Offer Flowers to the Rebels that Failed, 1973), a novel which, as the title suggests, deals with the failed hopes of the 1968 counterculture for radical change. Poet Pere Gimferrer's only novelistic excursion, *Fortuny* (1983), winner of the 1983 Ramon Llull prize, is in the words of Arthur Terry 'a series of impressions linked together by the history of the real life Fortuny family' rather than a novel in the conventional sense.[14]

There is, however, a limit to transgression, according to Àlex Broch, and that limit is linguistic. To cross the linguistic divide is 'passar al no-res dins la literatura catalana' ('to go beyond the pale of Catalan literature').[15] One such writer who did just that was Terenci Moix — the *bête noir* of Catalan letters — who in the 1960s and 1970s penned a number of extraordinary novels, including *El dia que va morir Marilyn* (The Day that Marilyn Died, 1969), which challenged the bourgeois sensibilities that dominated Catalan literature to that point via the frank and sympathetic treatment of homosexuality. In 1986, however, Moix became a 'deserter' and switched to writing in Castilian, only returning to the Catalan fold to write *El sexe dels àngels* (The Sex of Angels, 1992) and to publish a definitive edition of *El dia que va morir Marilyn* in 1996, as it had been substantially cut by the Francoist censors.

For Montserrat Roig, the existence of Catalans who write in Castilian, including some of the most important authors writing in the Iberian peninsula — such as Juan and Luis Goytisolo, Juan Marsé, Manuel Vázquez Montalbán, Eduardo Mendoza, and more recently, Nuria Amat and Carlos Ruiz Zafón — as well as the near impossibility of making a living from writing exclusively in Catalan, is evidence of a 'crisi d'identitat' ('identity crisis').[16] At the centre of this crisis is the question of who can be considered a Catalan writer and what can be recognised as a work of Catalan literature, a polemical debate that rears its head every couple of years, most recently at the 2007 Frankfurt Book Fair, at which Catalan culture was the 'guest of honour'.[17] As part of the *Congrés de Cultura Catalana* (Conference on Catalan Culture) which took place in 1976-1977, the *Primer Encontre d'Escriptors dels Països Catalans* (the First Meeting of Writers from the Catalan-Speaking Lands) somewhat unsurprisingly sought to resolve the issue by describing Catalan writers as 'els qui escriuen i/o publiquen llurs obres de creació en català' ('those who write or publish their creative works in Catalan').[18] As a consequence, with few exceptions, most studies of Catalan literature only examine literary works in Catalan.

Castilian-language writing from Catalonia indirectly provoked another major debate in Catalan literary circles — one concerning so-called urban versus rural literature. The critic Isidor Cònsul noted that 'no és difícil adonar-se que, actualment, la novel·la de Barcelona s'escriu en castellà' ('it's not hard to realise that currently the novel of Barcelona is written in Castilian') and there was the sense that Catalan-language writers needed to reclaim this urban space from the likes of Juan Marsé, Eduardo Mendoza and Manuel Vázquez Montalbán.[19] This led to a division between urban and rural writers, a division which has a long history in Catalan literary studies.[20]

As Kathryn Crameri notes in her introduction to this collection, the rural tag often implies a nostalgic, backward-looking, conservative outlook, whereas so-called urban literature is progressive, modern, and forward-looking. 'Rural' literature came to be personified in the figures of Jesús Moncada and Maria Barbal. Given that Moncada is the subject of this study, I shall focus on Barbal. As Brad Epps has shown, Barbal's designation as a 'rural' writer is not entirely accurate.[21] Through what is known as the Pallars cycle — *Pedra de tartera* (Stone of Debris, 1985), *Mel i metzines,* (Honey and Poison, 1990) and *Càmfora* (Camphor, 1992) — Barbal charts the difficult multiple transitions undertaken by rural Catalan speakers as they leave their villages and towns and, like so many Catalans during the second half of the twentieth century, migrate to urban centres, such as Barcelona, Paris and Caracas. Although the focus has been on Moncada and Barbal, numerous other writers set their works in rural settings. For example, Josep Albanell sets his *Ventada de morts* (A Deathly Gust of Wind, 1978) in the fictitious village Escornaldiable in the pre-Pyrenean region of Urgell. Others include Pep Coll and Emili Teixidor, who published respectively *Quan Judes era fadrí i la seva mare festejava* (When Judas was an Adolescent and his

Mother was Dating, 1986) and *Retrat d'un assassí d'ocells* (Portrait of a Bird Killer, 1988).

To say that Barcelona is largely represented in Castilian is incorrect. Many of the writers discussed here, including Montserrat Roig, Mercè Rodoreda, Terenci Moix, Jaume Fuster, Maria Jaén, Lluís-Maria Todó, and so on, set their works in the Catalan capital.[22] Nevertheless, the Catalan 'urban' writer *per excel·lència* is the novelist, short story writer and columnist Quim Monzó. Although he has written several novels, including *Benzina* (*Gasoline*, 1983), set in New York, and *La magnitud de la tragèdia* (*The Enormity of the Tragedy*, 1989), the latter a comedy about a man whose erection won't subside, Monzó is best known as a writer of short stories. Of his seven collections of short stories, the most significant are *Uf, va dir ell* (Oof, He Said, 1978), *Olivetti, Moulinex, Chaffoteaux et Maury* (*O'Clock*, 1980), *El perquè de tot plegat* (The Reason for Everything, 1993). Influenced by the modern masters of the genre — Coover, Barth, Cabrera Infante and Cortázar — Monzó explores in his short fiction the interaction between desire, the often twisted nature of relations between men and women, and the ways in which modern, urban life impedes individual happiness.

Often compared to Monzó, Sergi Pàmies has published several well-received collections of short stories including *T'hauria de caure la cara de vergonya* (You Should Hang your Head in Shame, 1986), *Infecció* (Infection, 1987) and the ironically titled *La gran novel·la sobre Barcelona* (The Great Novel about Barcelona, 1997), which is perhaps Pàmies's tongue-in-cheek final word on the pressure placed on Catalan-language writers to produce the definitive novel of the Catalan capital to rival their Castilian-language colleagues.

So-called urban literature is also closely associated with the development of popular literary forms in Catalan. The need to create popular fiction texts was particularly pertinent to Catalonia, given that the Franco regime had indirectly shaped the sort of literature that Catalans wrote. Faced with the fear of Catalan being considered an inferior language during the dictatorship, Catalan writers sought to 'maintain the prestige of Catalan as a language of high culture [... and] to prepare the ground for expansion in the post-Franco period' by producing works of high literature.[23] This focus on high-cultural forms led to Catalan culture being described in Joaquim Molas's memorable phrase as a 'gran cap sense cos. O, almenys, un gran cap amb un cos miserable i raquític' ('a big head without a body. Or, at the very least, a big head with a miserable and rickety body').[24]

To overcome the fact that during the 1970s and early 1980s readership in Catalan was limited to the well-educated, numerous writers sought to introduce popular genres into Catalan fiction, such as crime, erotica, romance, horror and science fiction, children's literature and even westerns in an attempt to attract readers to Catalan literature. Manuel de Pedrolo, a prolific author of 16 avant-garde plays, 16 books of poetry, 75 novels and 14 novellas or collections of short stories, was the principle promoter of genre fiction as a means of encouraging 'uns centenars, uns milers i tot, de lectors, ara poc familiaritzats amb el català escrit i massa mandrosos per a lliurar-se a l'esforç que, a llur entendre, suposa el fet d'abordar un llibre de més tonatge literari' ('several hundred, even thousands of readers, who are now not familiar with written Catalan and too lazy to make the effort that, in their opinion, is required to tackle a weightier work of literature').[25] During the dictatorship, Pedrolo published a series of crime novels and he was largely responsible for the development of contemporary science fiction in Catalan with the publication of *Mecanoscrit del segon origen* (Typescript of the Second Beginning, 1974), which has become one of the most read Catalan books of all time. This apocalyptic novel narrates the actions taken by two Catalan adolescents — Alba and Dídac — who survived the destruction of the world by aliens. As Alba's name — Dawn — suggests,

Pedrolo sees his protagonist as the founder of a new civilisation.

The development of popular fictions took a collective bent when several authors, including Jaume Fuster, Maria-Antònia Oliver, Antoni Serra, Pep Albanell and Jaume Cabré, among others, experimented with writing genre fiction under the pseudonym Ofèlia Dracs, including erotic fiction with *Deu pometes té el pomer* (The Apple Tree has Ten Little Apples, 1980), horror fiction with *Lovecraft, Lovecraft* (1981), crime fiction with *Negra i consentida* (Black and Hardboiled, 1983), and science fiction with *Essa efa* (SF, 1985). The aim of this collective, according to one of its members, Maria-Antònia Oliver, was to write 'popular' fictions that would resonate with the Catalan reading public so that 'readers did not have to go to translations or to Spanish books to get what their own culture was not offering them'.[26]

Of these genres, it is the crime novel which has been the most popular. The genre's success in Catalonia can be attributed primarily to the efforts of Jaume Fuster, a Barcelonan writer and critic, whose crime novels and short stories, including *De mica en mica s'omple la pica* (Little by Little the Sink Fills, 1972), *Les claus de vidre* (The Glass Keys, 1984), his homage to Dashiell Hammett and Ross MacDonald, and *Sota el signe de Sagitari* (Under the Sign of Saggitarius, 1986) quickly became bestsellers. The popularity of the crime novel stems from a belief that the genre seemed to encapsulate the mood of the transition: the increased violence, corruption, and political disillusionment when the return of democracy did not fulfil the high hopes placed on it by the citizenry after the long years of the dictatorship.[27] Fuster blazed the path for numerous other authors to write crime fiction. Andreu Martín, who began writing in Castilian, writes well-plotted novels of urban terror in Castilian as well as Catalan. Ferran Torrent offers a Valencian perspective with his series of novels protagonised by Butxana, including *No emprenyis el comissari* (Don't Piss Off the Commissioner, 1984). Mallorca too has its crime writers, including Antoni Serra and Maria-Antònia Oliver, whose three novels featuring the sassy Lonia Guiu have all been translated into English: *Estudi en lila* (*A Study in Lilac*, 1991), *Antípodes* (*Antipodes*, 1993), and *El sol que fa l'ànec* (*Blue Roses for a Dead... Lady*, 1994).

At the same time as Moncada was making his mark with so-called rural literature, erotic fiction in Catalan became mainstream with Maria Jaén's best-selling novella *Amorrada al piló* (Lips to the Microphone, 1986) which tells the story of Marta, a radio announcer on a late-night programme, who regales her listeners with erotic tales. The novel blurs the boundaries between fiction and reality, as readers are unsure what constitutes Marta's radio performance and her own sexual exploits at times during the broadcast itself. Jaén published another erotic novel, *Sauna* (1987), before writing more mainstream narratives (see below).

The abolition of censorship in 1977 allowed for the frank depiction of homosexuality in Catalan literature. Lluís Fernàndez published *L'anarquista nu* (*The Naked Anarchist*, 1979), an epistolary novel which recreates the Valencian gay scene through the letters that its members write to an absent friend. An academic and literary translator from French, Lluís-Maria Todó sees the period of the Transition to Democracy as a moment of gay liberation in his *El joc del mentider* (The Lying Game, 1994), a novel which, based on a popular dice game in which players progressively try to convince others that they are telling the truth, explores the construction of personal and sexual identities through role play.

Writing by women has flourished since the end of the dictatorship and works by Montserrat Roig, Carme Riera and Maria Barbal, among others, while not always attracting the attention of the critics, have become bestsellers. The Valencian writer Manuel Vicent's infamous quip that Montserrat Roig 'brought to literature [...] a pair of nice legs' is an example of the early dismissive attitude towards women's writing after

Franco.[28] Needless to say, Roig's contribution to Catalan literature was much more than her legs. In a series of novels and short stories, including *Ramona, adéu* (Farewell, Ramona 1972), *Els temps de les cireres* (Cherry Season, 1977) and *L'hora violeta* (The Violet Hour, 1980), Roig narrated the different fortunes facing Catalan women as both women and Catalans from the late nineteenth century until the Transition to Democracy through various members of the Miralpeix family. Roig was also one of the earliest Catalan writers to represent sympathetically the plight of Castilian-speaking immigrants to Catalonia in her collection of short stories, *Molta roba i poc sabó... i tan neta com la volen* (Lots of Washing, Not Much Soap, but as Clean as You Want It, 1971), and novels *L'òpera quotidiana* and *La veu melodiosa* (The Melodious Voice, 1987). In her short life (1946-1991) Roig became a major literary figure, publishing novels, short stories, and several important journalistic works, such as *Els catalans als camps nazis* (The Catalans in Nazi Concentration Camps, 1977).

Maria Jaén, herself born in Seville, also tackles the topic of immigration in *La dona discreta* (The Discreet Woman, 1997). This novel about the immigrant experience as told by the adult daughter of two Andalusian migrants to Catalonia is an unusual novel in Catalan letters, given that traditionally the stories of post-war immigrants are represented in Castilian.[29] It is even more remarkable because Jaén avoids the usual Catalan-Castilian linguistic and cultural conflict depicted in such novels by representing the entire text in Catalan. After writing the Pallars cycle, Maria Barbal published *Carrer Bolívia* (Bolivia Street, 1999) which, like *La dona discreta*, represents Andalusian immigration to Barcelona.

The Mallorcan writer and academic, Carme Riera, mixed lyricism, linguistic experimentation and gender politics in her early short stories. The title story to *Te deix, amor, la mar com a penyora* (I Leave You, My Love, the Sea as a Token, 1975) takes the form of a letter written by a female student to her teacher, with whom she had had an affair. Riera turns the stereotypical story of teacher-student love on its head in the last paragraph of the eighteen-page short story in which she reveals the teacher's gender, an impressive linguistic feat, given that Catalan nouns and adjectives are gender inflected. Riera also treats the theme of female sexuality in *Epitelis tendríssims* (Extremely Sensitive Skin, 1981), a collection of erotic tales set in a hotel in Deià, on Mallorca's west coast. More recently, Riera has written a number of works which could be described as historical novels, all of which employ sophisticated narrative techniques, such as multiple points of view, temporal jumps, and metafictional elements. *Dins el darrer blau* (In the Last Blue, 1994) tells of the persecution against a group of Jews in seventeenth-century Mallorca while *Cap al cel obert* (Towards the Open Sky, 2000) tells the story of one of the descendants of the Mallorcan Jews who seeks personal freedom in colonial Cuba around the middle of the nineteenth century. In addition to her crime fiction, Maria-Antònia Oliver writes about the effects of tourism and Castilianisation on her native Mallorca in *Crineres de foc* (Manes of Fire, 1984).

More recently, Empar Moliner and Imma Monsó have obtained critical and public recognition for their novels and short story collections. Monsó, in particular, has been described as 'una de les veus més sòlides i innovadores de la narrativa catalana contemporània' ('one of the most solid and innovative voices in contemporary Catalan narrative').[30] Born in Mequinensa, the same town as Moncada, Monsó burst onto the Catalan literary scene in her late thirties with the publication of *No se sap mai* (You Never Know, 1996) and during the period covered in this chapter Monsó published two more novels — *Com unes vacances* (Like Being on Holiday, 1998) and *Tot un caràcter* (What a Character, 2001) — and two short story collections — *Si és no és* (A Little Bit, 1997) and *Millor que no m'ho expliquis* (You'd Better Not Tell Me, 2003) — all of which have received critical praise and have generated impressive sales. Indeed, Monsó is one of the few Catalan-language writers, who, through the Castilian translations of her work, has become a bestseller throughout Spain.[31] This success in Catalan and Castilian is due to her fiction's ironic take on contemporary European society and values as well as her tender treatment of such difficult topics as cancer.

Maria-Àngels Anglada explores whether women's lives can ever be known in *Les closes* (The Enclosed, 1979) in which a young woman tries to discover the truth about her great-grandmother, Dolors Canals, who was accused and tried for the murder of her husband. In this attempted recreation of Dolors's life in the period prior to Spain's First Republic (1873-1874), the novel combines elements of oral history, personal testimony, newspaper clippings, court reports and household inventories, thus highlighting the difficulties in reclaiming women's history. Ultimately, the novel demonstrates that history is little more than interpretation of past events and that the past cannot truly be known.

Given that the Franco regime strictly policed how history was told and taught, the regime's end meant that writers were free to explore historical themes which had been previously taboo topics.[32] Teresa Pàmies, who, as an adolescent had been a communist militant in Balaguer and who had lived in exile, published a series of testimonial novels and memoirs about her experiences during the Spanish Civil War, including *Va ploure tot el dia* (It Rained All Day, 1974) and *Quan érem capitans* (When We Were in Charge, 1974). Other writers sought to explain Catalonia's subjugation within the Spanish state, such as Ramon Pallicé with *Cap de brot* (The Leader, 1982), which tells of Catalan resistance to the forces of Philip V following the War of Spanish Succession (1701-1714). This war, which gave Catalonia its national day — 11 September — is also the subject of Alfred Bosch's best-selling trilogy, consisting of *1714, Set de rey* (1714, Thirst for Royalty, 2002), *1714, Sota la pell del diable* (1714, Under the Devil's Skin, 2002) and *1714, Toc de vespres* (1714, Night Call, 2002).

Catalonia's medieval past has also been a rich source of stories for writers like Lluís Racionero, whose *Cercamón* (He Who Travels the World, 1982), winner of the 1981 Prudenci Bertrana prize, tells the story — through the eyes of a young troubadour — of Catalonia's failure to conceive and maintain a trans-Pyrenean Catalan nation and with it the rejection of the tradition of courtly love and tolerance in favour of expanding Catalan influence in Mallorca and Valencia during the reign of James I 'The Conqueror'. The Conqueror is also the subject of Andorran Albert Salvadó's 2001 novel *Jaume 1, el conqueridor*. Other famous Catalans, such as the nineteenth-century poet-priest Jacint Verdaguer and the Mallorcan mystic Ramon Llull, have also had their lives novelised by Valencian Isabel-Clara Simó — *Mossèn* (Father, 1987) — and Francesc Puigpelat — *L'últim hivern de Ramon Llull* (Ramon Llull's Last Winter, 2004).

The effect of the industrial revolution on Catalonia and the Catalan-speaking area has been the subject of several novels by Jaume Cabré and Isabel-Clara Simó, among others. Cabré published the 'Feixes' trilogy — *La teranyina* (The Cobweb 1983), *Fra Junoy o l'agonia dels sons* (Father Junoy, or the Agony of Dreams, 1983) and *Luvowski o la desraó* (Luvowski, or the Lack of Reason, 1985) — and Simó, whose work explores what it means to be a woman, working-class and a Catalan speaker, published *Júlia* (1983), which recounts the struggle of the labour movement in Valencia at the turn of the twentieth century. Cabré has recently joined Quim Monzó and Maria Barbal as a best-selling author in Germany, following former Minister of Foreign Affairs and leader of the German Green Party, Joschka Fischer's enthusiastic endorsement of *Les veus del Pamano* (The Pamano Voices, 2004) at the 2007 Frankfurt Book Fair. This novel about the Francoist repression in the Pyrenean region of Pallars engages with the question of historical memory, justice and how we can understand the past from the perspective of the present. Cabré's novels are renowned for their narrative complexity, different voices and timeframes, making him one of Catalonia's most critically acclaimed and best-selling contemporary authors.

The other darling of the Frankfurt Book Fair was anthropologist and novelist Albert Sánchez Piñol, who has written a series of novels and short stories about Africa and humanity's tendency to resort to violence when encountering the Other. *La pell freda* (*Cold Skin*, 2003) is a horror novel in the Lovecraftian tradition in which the protagonist — a weatherman fleeing Europe for reasons which remain unclear — ends up on a small, remote Antarctic island where he is beset by beastly sea creatures which he must kill in order to survive. Strange beasts also appear in *Pandora al Congo* (*Pandora in the Congo*, 2005), Sánchez Piñol's postmodern adventure cum horror cum detective novel set in pre-World War I is based on any number of imperial adventure stories, including Conrad's *Heart of Darkness*. Sánchez Piñol's works, with their focus on non-Catalan topics, illustrate perhaps the distance that Catalan literature has covered since the defensive days under the Franco regime when writers felt they had to tell stories which were essentially about Catalans and Catalonia.

Catalan literature has come a long way since the last years of the Franco regime, as there is little doubt that since 1970 many excellent works have been produced by Catalan, Mallorcan and Valencian writers, including, among others, Baltasar Porcel, Montserrat Roig, Quim Monzó, Carme Riera, Isabel-Clara Simó, Jaume Cabré, Imma Monsó, Albert Sánchez Piñol and, of course, the subject of this collection, Jesús Moncada. This period has also seen the development and boom of popular fiction forms and women's writing, both of which had been largely under-represented in Catalan letters. Thus, despite lamentations about the quality of contemporary Catalan literature by some cultural commentators, such weeping and wailing about its imminent demise is — to borrow from Mark

Twain — greatly exaggerated. Indeed, the number and the diversity of works being published highlight that whereas Catalan literature may once have been a withered body with a big head (*pace* Joaquim Molas), since 1970 this body has grown stronger, and this can only be good for the health of Catalan literature into the future.

Notes

[1] Carolyn P. Boyd, 'History, Politics, and Culture, 1936-1975', in *The Cambridge Companion to Modern Spanish Culture*, ed. by David T. Gies (Cambridge: Cambridge University Press, 1999), 86-103, p. 86.

[2] Daniele Conversi, *The Basques, the Catalans and Spain: Alternative Routes to Nationalist Mobilisation* (London: Hurst & Company, 1997), p. 111.

[3] Kathryn Woolard, *Double Talk: Bilingualism and the Politics of Ethnicity in Catalonia* (Stanford: Stanford University Press, 1989), p. 33. Woolard's figure of 50% refers to Catalan speakers generally throughout Catalonia and does not take into account that in individual regions the figure was either much higher or much lower.

[4] Josep-Anton Fernàndez, *El malestar en la cultura catalana. La cultura de la normalització 1976-1999* (Barcelona: Empúries, 2008), p. 38. All translations into English in this chapter are by Stewart King.

[5] For a very personal view of the importance of TV3 for the normalisation process, see Quim Monzó, 'Mirror, Mirror on the Wall', in *Catalonia: A Self-Portrait*, ed. by Josep Miquel Sobrer (Bloomington: Indiana University Press, 1992), pp. 65-6.

[6] Ferran Carbó and Vicent Simbor, *Literatura catalana del siglo XX* (Madrid: Síntesis, 2005), pp. 253, 254.

[7] Although this number includes publications written in Castilian and published in Catalonia, the overwhelming majority of prizes are works in Catalan (or Aranese). For more on the question of literary prizes see Kathryn Crameri, *Catalonia: National Identity and Cultural Policy, 1980-2003* (Cardiff: University of Wales Press, 2008), pp. 90-2.

[8] Carles-Jordi Guardiola, *Ofici d'editar* (Barcelona: La Magrana, 1996), p. 42.

[9] See J-A. Fernàndez, *El malestar*, pp. 202-17.

[10] Guillem-Jordi Graells and Oriol Pi de Cabanyes, *La generació literària dels 70* (Barcelona: Pòrtic, 1971), p. 11. See also Kathryn Crameri,

Language, the Novelist and National Identity in Post-Franco Catalonia (Oxford: Legenda, 2000), pp. 69-76.

[11] Àlex Broch, *Literatura catalana dels anys 70* (Barcelona: Edicions 62, 1980), p. 104.

[12] Baltasar Porcel, 'Who I Am and Why I Write', *Lletra: Catalan Literature on line*. Available on http://www.lletra.net/noms/bporcel/index.html (accessed on 2/4/2010).

[13] For a detailed analysis of Mesquida's work, see Crameri, *Language*, pp. 116-55, and Josep-Anton Fernàndez, *Another Country: Sexuality and National Identity in Catalan Gay Fiction* (Leeds: Maney, 2000), pp. 165-87.

[14] Arthur Terry, *A Companion to Catalan Literature* (London: Tamesis, 2003), p. 136.

[15] Broch, p. 112.

[16] Montserrat Roig in Jordi Carbonell, 'Escriure en castellà a Catalunya', *Taula de canvi*, 6, 1977, 5-42, p. 35. For more on this issue, see the various contributions to *La cultura catalana de expresión castellana. Estudios de literatura, teatro y cine*, ed. by Stewart King (Kassel: Reichenberger, 2005).

[17] For an analysis of these debates, see Stewart King, 'Catalan Literature(s) in Postcolonial Context', *Romance Studies*, 24, 3, 2006, pp. 253-64; and Stewart King, 'From Literature to Letters: Rethinking Catalan Literary History, in *New Spain, New Literatures*, ed. by Luis Martín-Estudillo and Nicholas Spadaccini (Nashville: Vanderbilt University Press, 2010), pp. 233-44.

[18] *Congrés de cultura catalana. Vol. 2 Resolucions*. ([Barcelona]: Països Catalans, 1978), p. 309. For a discussion of the Congrés de Cultura Catalana, see Crameri, *Catalonia*, pp. 31-2.

[19] Isidor Cònsul, 'Geografies mítiques', *Lletra de canvi*, 31-2, 1990, 8-12, p. 11.

[20] See Víctor Martínez-Gil, '*De re urbana* i *de re rurali*, un altre cop?', *Els marges*, 44, 1991, pp. 61-5.

[21] Brad Epps, 'Moving in Tongues: Immigration and Language in Maria Barbal', in *Beyond the Periphery: Narratives of Identity in the Basque Country, Catalonia and Galicia*, ed. by Stewart King, a special number of *Antípodas: Journal of Hispanic and Galician Studies*, 18, 2007, pp. 101-31.

[22] For an in-depth analysis of literature and Barcelona, see *Narrativas urbanas. La construcción literaria de Barcelona*, ed. by Margarida Casacuberta and Marina Gustà (Barcelona: Fundació Antoni Tàpies, 2008), and Marta E. Altisent, 'Images of Barcelona', in *A Companion to*

the Twentieth-Century Spanish Novel, ed. by Marta E. Altisent (Woodbridge: Tamesis, 2008), pp. 137-57.

[23] Josep-Anton Fernàndez, 'Becoming Normal: Cultural Production and Cultural Policy in Catalonia', in *Spanish Cultural Studies: An Introduction. The Struggle for Modernity*, ed. by Helen Graham and Jo Labanyi (Oxford: Oxford University Press, 1995), 342-6, pp. 342-3.

[24] Joaquim Molas, 'La cultura catalana i la seva estratificació', in *Reflexions crítiques sobre la cultura catalana*, ed. by P. Vilar et al (Barcelona: Generalitat de Catalunya, 1983), 131-55, p. 154.

[25] A.M.,'Enquesta: La novel·la policíaca a Catalunya', *Serra d'Or* 3, 1961, 13-14, p. 13.

[26] Patricia Hart, 'The Mystery as Midwife: An Interview with Maria-Antònia Oliver', *The Armchair Detective* (Summer 1992), 330-34, p. 332.

[27] José F. Colmeiro, 'Spanish Detective Fiction as a Political Genre', in *A Companion to the Twentieth-Century Spanish Novel*, ed. by Marta E. Altisent (Woodbridge: Tamesis, 2008), 114-26, p. 117.

[28] Cited in Catherine Davies, *Contemporary Feminist Fiction in Spain: The Work of Montserrat Roig and Rosa Montero* (Oxford: Berg, 1994), p. ix.

[29] For a detailed analysis of literary representations of post-war immigration to Catalonia, see Stewart King, *Escribir la catalanidad. Lengua e identidades culturales en la narrativa contemporánea de Cataluña* (London: Tamesis, 2005), pp. 86-110.

[30] Montserrat Lunati Maruny, *Imma Monsó: la narrativa de la ironia i la diferència* (Vic: Eumo/Universitat de Vic, 2007), p. 19.

[31] Lunati Maruny, p. 29.

[32] For a discussion of historical studies during the Franco regime, see David Herzberger, *Narrating the Past: Fiction and Historiography in Postwar Spain* (Durham: Duke University Press, 1995).

Chapter 2

Jesús Moncada: A Biographical Sketch
Hèctor Moret

Jesús Moncada i Estruga was born in Mequinensa, in the county of Baix Cinca, in the Catalan-speaking part of Aragón now known as La Franja, on the first of December 1941. This was the toughest and most sinister stage in the postwar period, and the town — which at that time had a population of around 3,500 — had been decisively defeated. Moncada was born into a family of shopkeepers whose roots in this area went back many centuries. Mequinensa, situated at the confluence of the rivers Segre and Ebro (the river with the greatest flow of water in the whole of the Iberian Peninsula), had been for almost all of the twentieth century something of an oddity in the context of the region's agrarian economy. This was because of the commercial and — especially — industrial character of its own economy, which was based on the mining of lignite from numerous mines that were scattered around the municipality, and its transportation downriver to the railway station at Faió. This also made for a particular kind of social relations in the town, which was mainly made up of craftsmen, shopkeepers, salaried workers (miners and bargees) and the businessmen who owned the mines and barges. Only a small number of people worked on the land, and even fewer were shepherds or cattle farmers.

In 1953, once he had finished his primary education in his home town, Moncada (who was not yet twelve) had to move to Zaragoza (the capital both of the region of Aragón and the province within which Mequinensa is situated) in order to complete the last two years of his elementary *Bachillerato*, and then the higher level of that qualification, at the school run by the Labordeta family. The Saint Thomas Aquinas School was unusual amongst the secondary schools in Zaragoza at that time because it was liberal and not run by the Church. Amongst its teachers of language and literature were the poet Miguel Labordeta, the writer, poet and literary critic Rosendo Tello, and, at the start of his teaching career, the future singer-songwriter, writer and politician José Antonio Labordeta. Despite Mequinensa's proximity to Lleida — the economic and social capital of the whole of the Baix Cinca area and the rest of the Northern and Central counties of Catalan-speaking Aragón — at that time the Catalan city only had boarding schools controlled by religious communities, which were not suitable according to Jesús's quite liberal, non-religious and republican father.

In Zaragoza, Jesús Moncada found himself surrounded by a culture and, above all, a language (Castilian, which he already knew quite well but only from his books and studies) that was different from his maternal language, Catalan. On more than one occasion he was the object of ridicule and scorn from his classmates when they heard him speak in Catalan with friends and relatives from Mequinensa. He never felt fully at home in the city, so it is no surprise that whenever he had the opportunity (mostly the school holidays) he would return to Mequinensa to flee from this sense of emotional exile.

At the same time as finishing the last courses in the higher *Bachillerato* Moncada was also getting on with the three-year teaching course at the *Escuela Normal* in the Aragonese capital. At the age of 17 he returned to Mequinensa a fully-qualified teacher, spending a couple of years as a primary school teacher before he had to return to Zaragoza to perform compulsory military service. Once this was over, he returned to Mequinensa to teach for a short while in a middle school.

In 1966 Moncada, like many of his fellow Mequinensans at that time, decided to move to Barcelona, where he met the journalist, translator and historian Edmon Vallès i Pedrix (Mequinensa 1920 — Barcelona 1980), who was to provide him with help and encouragement in a variety of ways. After spending a year as a commercial painter, working with the artist Santiago Estruga Aliaga (Mequinensa 1910 — Barcelona 2004), Jesús Moncada took a job at the publishers Montaner y Simón as an assistant to the production manager Pere Calders — the great Catalan writer who had returned from exile in Mexico in 1962 — who would also encourage him to write and with whom he would maintain a close friendship.

One of the key reasons for moving to the capital of Catalonia was his desire to gain exposure outside the confines of his home region for his art works, of which there was already a vast number, and his incipient literary creation. Moncada had always dedicated himself intensively and simultaneously to painting, reading and literary reflection. In fact, his creative trajectory was to begin, at least consciously, with the exhibition of his works of art. In 1966 and 1970 he exhibited some of his work in venues in Mequinensa, and in the second half of the seventies he took part in both individual and collective exhibitions in different locations around Catalonia: Mataró (1977 and 1978), Barcelona (1977 and 1978), Vilassar de Mar (1979), etc. The last exhibition in which Moncada showed his art work took place at the Caixa d'Estalvis Laietana in Arenys de Mar in 1980. However, it was precisely at the beginning of the eighties, at the same time as the publication of his first collection of short stories *Històries de la mà esquerra i altres narracions* (Stories of the Left Hand and other Tales, 1981) and, more importantly, the death of his father in 1982, that Moncada decided to give up painting and devote more time to his literary creation.

The start of the 1980s also saw the closure of the publishing company Montaner y Simón where Moncada had worked for thirteen years. This had the side effect of allowing him to dedicate himself fully to his writing, although he did have to balance his nascent career as a writer with work, including translations, for different Catalan publishers. This continued to be the pattern of his career until the appearance of the first symptoms of a serious illness in the summer of 2004, which was eventually diagnosed in mid-October of the same year, and which led to his death in a Barcelona clinic on 13 June 2005.

Discovery and learning of the written language

While he was already teaching in Mequinensa, at the beginning of the sixties, Jesús Moncada was on a trip to Lleida when he discovered a shelf full of books in Catalan in an old bookshop. This surprised him: he had not known that Catalan existed as a literary language. We need to remind ourselves that at that time Moncada lived in an Aragonese town where, although Catalan was spoken on a daily basis, the authorities and the Francoist administration made every effort to ensure that the language had no literary outlet. The Castilian functionaries in the town, especially the schoolteachers, drummed into the population the idea that they were not speaking a proper language, Catalan, but a garbled mix of different languages and dialects — *chapurreado*, as they pejoratively insisted on calling it — that was tainted, half-caste and worthless and had no social or literary value whatsoever.

Since he was a teenager, Jesús Moncada had taken the time, in the spirit of a true researcher, to interview the shipwrights and bargees of Mequinensa about the characteristics of life on the river Ebro. He made notes in Castilian, but soon realised that this was not altogether satisfactory: he lacked an intimate link with the tool of his trade, and knew intuitively that there was a dichotomy between the thought expressed in oral language and that of the written word. So, when he discovered the translation into Catalan of *Le Cimetière marin* by Paul Valéry on the shelf of that bookshop in Lleida, he said to himself 'what's going on here'?

Moncada's journey towards Catalan as a literary language accelerated after a visit to the town by Edmon Vallès. 'You should write in Catalan', Vallès told him, aware of the young teacher's interest in literature, but Moncada was stumped by this: 'Oh, but is that possible?', he dared to respond. Realising Moncada's growing affection for their shared language, the Mequinensan historian sent him from Barcelona copies of works by Catalan writers and, especially, Catalan translations of authors from around the world. However, it was not until he moved to the capital of Catalonia that Moncada opted to use his maternal language in his literary work. Pere Calders (Barcelona, 1912-1994), who knew about Moncada's interest in writing through Vallès, asked to be allowed to read something he was writing, but Moncada had not yet written anything in Catalan. In three months he wrote — not without effort — the story 'Jocs de caps' ('Head Games'). Calders liked it a lot and encouraged him to continue.

Those literary beginnings were not at all easy for Moncada, since he came up against the difficulty of not having a good command of Catalan grammar or, more significantly, spelling. He was lucky that Calders acted as a kind of mentor to him, and patiently took on the task of pointing out and correcting the spelling mistakes in Moncada's nascent literary Catalan, although he encouraged him not to stop using the genuine linguistic peculiarities of the variety of Catalan spoken in Mequinensa.

First texts and literary prizes

Encouraged by Pere Calders — and Xavier Benguerel, Edmon Vallès and other regular visitors to Montaner y Simón — Jesús Moncada submitted his work to a few literary competitions. Just a few months apart he won the 1970 Brugués prize with the short story 'La lluna, la pruna' ('The Moon, the Prune') and obtained second prize in the competition for young writers run by the magazine *Serra d'Or* with the article 'Crònica del darer rom' ('Chronicle of the Last Rum'), in which some of the keys to the author's literary world can already be glimpsed, and which was published in the March 1971 edition of the journal. This was the first text ever published by Jesús Moncada. Two months later, in May 1971, he won the Joan Santamaria prize with four stories that were to be published in 1973 under the title of *Històries de la mà esquerra,* in a collective volume accompanied by two stories by Josep Vallverdú and Jaume Melendres, the other finalists in the competition. *Històries de la mà esquerra* was the first literary work by a Catalan writer born in Aragón to be published in book form.

The decade of the seventies was still a period of great activity for Moncada in creative art: between 1977 and 1980 he showed his work on at least six occasions. It would not be until 1980 that he would obtain the Jacme March prize from the town council of Gavà, with four stories that were given the title of *Narracions de l'Ebre* ('Stories of the Ebro'). He entered the competition with the encouragement of Josep Soler Vidal, an old and close friend from Montaner y Simón.

Històries de la mà esquerra

In 1981, Edicions La Magrana published *Històries de la mà esquerra i altres narracions,* with a prologue by Pere Calders. It groups together sixteen stories: the four that won the Joan Santamaria prize in 1970 under the title *Històries de la mà esquerra*, the four from *Narracions de l'Ebre* that won the Jacme March prize in 1980 (now with the title *La pell del riu* 'The Surface of the River'), and a third section entitled *Cròniques de la sirga* ('Chronicles of the Towpath') with the remaining eight stories, among which was 'La lluna, la pruna', which had won Moncada the 1970 Brugués prize.

The rather miscellaneous character of this first collection of short stories, which was no doubt the result of its long and intermittent gestation, was diluted in subsequent editions when the division into sections that we find in the first edition was abandoned and the phrase *i altres narracions* was dropped from the title. Despite this, the heterogeneous origin of the stories in the collection was still readily apparent. For example, of all the stories Jesús Moncada wrote, we see here the only three that have no connection, in one way or another, with the setting of Mequinensa: 'Conte del vell tramviaire' ('Tale of the Old Tram Driver'), 'L'estremidora confessió de Joe Galàxia' ('The Shocking Confession of Joe Galaxy') and 'Història de dies senars' ('The Story of Odd-Numbered Days'). In the thirteen remaining stories, even though they are set — with greater or lesser intensity — in Mequinensa, we do not find the name of the town explicitly mentioned, but replaced by names that have been created *ex professo* (e.g. Cantalaigua), or neutral appellations such as 'town'.

In some of the stories in this collection, as many critics have remarked (among them Xavier Moret), we can still see quite markedly the influence of Pere Calders, and in many of them we find a Fellinian atmosphere of nostalgia passed through a literary filter, half way between drama and comedy.

El Cafè de la Granota

Written between 1980 and 1985, the fourteen stories contained in this second collection — published in 1985 by Edicions La Magrana — have, thanks to their common setting, a clearly unitary character, especially when compared with the rather heterogeneous character of *Històries de la mà esquerra*. Even so, the unitary character of this second collection is not as strong, at least in regards to structure, as that of the last volume, *Calaveres Atònites* (Astonished Skulls), that was published fourteen years later in 1999.

Although it might seem that the stories that we find in the collection *El Cafè de la Granota* were not initially designed with the aim of forging a unity between them (i.e. the author had no initial plan for this), the final result, thanks to a suite of elements that impregnate all, or at least the majority, of the stories, is relatively homogeneous.

The first and most important element that helps to forge a sense of unity in the collection is the spatial setting in which the action of the stories takes place. This action has its epicentre, explicitly now, in the town of Mequinensa — with a few scarce references to the towns in its immediate vicinity -, in its cafés, streets and squares, in the mines of its municipality and in the barges moored to the jetties on the Ebro. The people who are portrayed here — bargees, miners, farmworkers, shopkeepers... — are almost always, whether masculine or feminine, inhabitants of the steep, cheerful and slow-paced town of Mequinensa.

Even though few facts are mentioned in the stories, the temporal and historic framework for the action can be located in the decade of the 1950s and the beginning of the 1960s, which also reinforces the unitary conception of this collection. It also serves to date the action of the stories, and perhaps even more clearly locates the atmosphere of repression and political oppression exuded by the stories, along with several explicit references to the dictatorship and Francoism that we find throughout the work.

A third element that further reinforces the impression that *El Cafè de la Granota* is a work with a great deal of homogeneity is the tone of humour and strong irony that impregnates most of the stories. Often the humour and irony in these short narratives — and in the rest of the stories — by Jesús Moncada is motivated by an unexpected event that, so to speak, subtly forces the logic of a situation that, at the outset, is perfectly ordinary. This humorous treatment is reminiscent of some of the best stories by Pere Calders, who was a master of the construction of narrations characterised by subtlety and stylistic suggestiveness. Death and funeral rituals also often receive from Moncada a treatment full of irony and humour that reduces their transcendence and makes them seem part of the everyday.

Almost as if they were medieval *exempla* with a didactic, edifying or warning function, on occasions Moncada seems to have written some of the stories in *El Cafè de la Granota* to illustrate — critically but humorously — the passions, moral attitudes, desires and dreams of different characters (of course, without any moral or — even less — religious intention). They contain a social critique that allows the personal sympathies of the author to show through and that on occasions borders on satire. In the case of socially disadvantaged characters this is usually accompanied by a measure of tenderness that takes some of the intensity away from the criticism. On the other hand, if the criticism is aimed at a character from the wealthy or powerful classes the narration has a more penetrating edge, with a touch of sarcasm or corrosive irony.

Camí de sirga

With the novel *Camí de sirga,* published by Edicions La Magrana in 1988, the name of Jesús Moncada comes to stand out in the Catalan literature of the last two decades of the twentieth century. The work merited the almost unanimous approval of the critics and ample acknowledgement on the part of the readers.

This extensive and dense novel, structured around four parts and an epilogue, has often been described as a choral novel. In it, the history of almost a century in the life of Mequinensa — and the Catalan Ebro — is portrayed, thanks to the presence of a series of characters and a constant switching from past to present, from present to past; a to-ing and fro-ing that encompasses a broad period of time that starts just before the beginning of the First World War and ends in 1971, the year in which the slow annihilation of Mequinensa began once the construction of the Riba-Roja reservoir, downstream on the Ebro, was completed. The list of the prizes garnered by this novel is long, but needs to be mentioned: Joan Crexells (1988), Fundació d'Amics de les Arts i de les Lletres de Sabadell (1988), Nacional de la Crítica (1988), Ciutat de Barcelona (1989), Crítica Serra d'Or (1989); it was also a finalist in the Premio Nacional de Literatura (1988).

International recognition also came swiftly, which means that to date *Camí de sirga* has been translated into sixteen languages: German (1995), English (1994), Aragonese (2003), Spanish (1989), Danish (1993), Slovenian (2004), French (1992), Galician (1997), Hungarian (2005), Japanese (1999), Dutch (1992), Portuguese (1992), Romanian (1997), Serbian (2007), Swedish (1996) and Vietnamese (1996).

La galeria de les estàtues

The second novel by Jesús Moncada, published in 1992 also by Edicions La Magrana in Barcelona, is another plural work, although less choral than *Camí de sirga*, which contains a wide range of characters. The linking thread of 'The Statue Gallery' is the story of Dalmau Campells, a young student from Mequinensa training to be a teacher in Torrelloba, a city in the interior of the Peninsula that the author defines as 'més gran que Lleida [i] també més que Saragossa' ('bigger than Lleida [and] also bigger than Zaragoza'),[1] but any attentive reader will identify it easily with the capital of Aragón thanks to the atmosphere and the morphology of the city as it is described in the novel. The historical setting is the end of the 1950s; more specifically, the narration starts on 27 November 1957 and ends on the 12 December of the same year, the period during which the war of Ifni was taking place, when the Spanish military confronted the inhabitants of this colonial enclave in the north of Africa. However, there are also numerous flashbacks that take the narrative back to the years of the Civil War. The action takes place in a series of comings and goings between the city and Mequinensa, with characters — priests, soldiers, policemen, administrators — who move through the setting of a Spanish provincial city that is decidedly grey and sad. Moncada sometimes said that he had put into the character of Dalmau Campells, the trainee teacher from Mequinensa, some autobiographical traits, but he never admitted that the Torrelloba of the novel was actually Zaragoza.

Estremida memòria

In this third novel, published in 1997 by Edicions La Magrana, Mequinensa and its inhabitants once more dominate — almost exclusively — the setting of the narration. A transcendental occurrence in the history of the town is apparently the central theme of the work: a case of banditry that occurred, as is indicated in the preamble that begins the novel, in the town between the months of August and November 1877 and that has endured in the memory and the oral tradition of the people of Mequinensa and the surrounding villages. In this kaleidoscopic novel, that is almost as choral as *Camí de sirga*, social and — especially — political repression are described without hesitation and with a hint of bitterness. Once more the collective memory of the Mequinensans (the 'jolted memory' that is referred to in the title of the work) has a prominent role in this novel.

Calaveres atònites

The clearly unitary character of the third collection of stories by Jesús Moncada, published in Barcelona by Edicions la Magrana in 1999, has meant that on occasions this book has understandably been called a quasi-novel, or a novel of characters, a view which is reinforced by the presence of a prologue and epilogue — both of them very false, or very literary — which act as a glue that reinforces the sense of unity between the fourteen stories that are included. The prologue and epilogue are narrated, respectively, through the eyes of a young and naive lawyer who has been posted to Mequinensa as the court secretary in the 1950s, and from the ironic and wise perspective of the local judge.

Cabòries estivals i altres proses volanderes

This slim volume ('Summer Worries and Other Restless Prose'), published in Calaceit in 2003 by various cultural associations from Catalan-speaking Aragón, brings together all Moncada's press articles, of which there are very few, as well as an unpublished story. The book starts with 'Crònica del darrer rom', the first publication by the author (in 1971), and ends with the unpublished 'Una estampa del segle XVII' ('A Seventeenth-Century Print'). Thirty-two years had passed between the first publications of the former and the latter, during which the writer from Mequinensa had produced a dense, subtle and precise corpus of literature that had been slowly and laboriously crafted.

General Characteristics

Jesús Moncada's writing, which was already in development in the 1960s and came to public attention from the 1970s onwards, is mostly centred (as the various commentators who have worked on it never cease to point out) on the urban and rural geography of Mequinensa; the history (both intimate and large-scale) of the town during the years that run, basically, from 1860 to 1971; and especially the behaviour and psychology of its inhabitants, past and present. This means that, as has already been said, of the forty-five short stories Moncada published — in three volumes that have now been brought together in *Contes* ('Stories', 2001) — only three are not set in one way or another in that particular town on the Ebro. Mequinensa is also the geographical and human setting in which Moncada's three novels unfold, almost exclusively in the first and third of these, while only partially, but to an important extent, in the second.

In order to understand this spatial and temporal dedication of the whole of Moncada's work we must take into account not only the socioeconomic uniqueness of Mequinensa — a town of proletarians (miners and bargees) and bourgeois, surrounded by agricultural villages — but also the many hours that the young Moncada spent in his parents' shop, in the numerous cafés that were scattered around the dynamic town of Mequinensa, or simply in its streets and squares. There he would hear from the mouths of the farm workers, miners, shipwrights and — especially — bargees of Mequinensa the stories, jokes and adventures (whether real or imagined) whose protagonists were often those very same miners or sailors. This was why the town of Mequinensa and the relationships between its inhabitants became the starting-point that, combined with an undeniable talent for narrative, an obvious thirst for reading and an inherent (although masterfully controlled) sense of imagination, would permit him to create a rich and nuanced literary universe — a microcosm — in which the collective memory of Mequinensa is the principal protagonist. This little universe has a basis in reality but also clear epic connotations, to the extent that it is not strange that there are those who see this universe as mythical: the myth of Mequinensa. A myth that, paradoxically, seems possible only as a result of the disappearance of the real Mequinensa: its old town centre, the tradition of sailing the Ebro, the decline of mining exports etc.; a disappearance that was caused by modern times, the important socio-economic transformations of the later years of the Franco regime, and most of all by the construction of the Riba-Roja and Mequinensa reservoirs along the Ebro, a waterway that up to that moment had been the backbone of life in Mequinensa and that, as Emili Bayo has said, takes on so much importance that it does not seem exaggerated to talk about it as a character within Moncada's fiction.[2]

Rather than the fact that the language used by Jesús Moncada reflects the vocabulary and phraseology of Western Catalan — and on occasion even local or regional forms, as is inevitably the case with a lot of the vocabulary related to the navigation of the Ebro —, perhaps the thing that most characterises the writer's literary language is orality, especially in the case of the short stories. They have a tone of oral language that make them seem as if the tales had been gathered directly from the voice of the townspeople. In fact, often the narrator presents himself as simply a scribe or chronicler who is trying to write down as faithfully as possible what the old Mequinensans have explained to him. These features of Moncada's style will be explored in more detail in the next chapter, which concentrates on his short stories.

Notes

[1] GE (Barcelona: La Magrana, 1992), p. 125.
[2] Emili Bayo, 'Jesús Moncada: La memòria més enllà de les aigües', in Emili Bayo and Mercè Biosca *Guia de lectura de Jesús Moncada* (Barcelona: Magrana, 1992), p. 43.

Chapter 3

The Short Stories:
The Universe and Voices of Mequinensa
Sandrine Ribes

Organisation and themes of the three collections of short stories

Jesús Moncada is the author of three books of short stories: *Històries de la mà esquerra* (1981), *El café de la Granota* (1985) and *Calaveres atònites* (1999). In fact he first entered the world of Catalan literature thanks to the publication of the first of these volumes, *Històries de la mà esquerra*.

This collection comprises sixteen stories written between 1970 and 1980. It was initially divided into three groups of texts. The first, *Històries de la mà esquerra*, opens the volume and provides its overall title; this group corresponds to the collection of stories that won the Joan Santamaria prize in 1971 and was first published in 1973 with hardly any publicity. The second section of the book contains the collection *La pell del riu* which, under the title of *Narracions de l'Ebre*, had received the 1980 Jacme March prize given by the town of Gavà. The story 'La lluna, la pruna', which obtained the Brugués prize in 1970, opens the third section which corresponds to the series of texts entitled *Cròniques de sirga*. The first complete edition came out in 1981 under the full title *Històries de la mà esquerra i altres narracions* in La Magrana's collection 'Les ales esteses'. In 1988 a new edition of the book appeared, in which the division into sections was eliminated at the request of the author himself.

With the exception of three of the texts,[1] the majority of the stories constitute a homogeneous group as far as the setting and themes are concerned. The principal location is the former municipality of Mequinensa, recreated by the author through the social and political circumstances his town had experienced since Spain's Second Republic. These stories are characterised by their alternation between the most trivial and ordinary details of daily life, and extraordinary or even fantastic elements. The unreal breaks through into the everyday: for example, the characters accept as normal the participation in village life of phantoms generated by the passing of time.

The author's second book, *El Cafè de la Granota*, appeared in 1985. It comprises fourteen stories written between 1980 and 1985 whose thematic continuity with the preceding volume allows them to be analysed together. In fact, the majority of the stories that have rural settings are characterised by their fatalism. The recurring theme of death (burials, wakes) is not treated with a tragic tone, but is de-dramatised and made humorous. In many cases this consists of a critical view of the hypocrisy of wakes and polite expressions of condolence, which are actually devoid of real emotion. In the story 'Senyora Mort, carta de Miquel Garrigues' ('Lady Death, a letter from Miquel Garrigues'), the classical myth of Charon is shattered by the innocent request from the boatman Miquel Garrigues that he should be employed in the next world as the skipper of the boat that crosses the river Lethe, transporting the souls of the dead from one shore to the other, so that he can replace Charon on public holidays. This mixture of the unspeakable (death) and the everyday, tragedy with comedy, is the key to the black humour that is found throughout Moncada's work but which, according to him, is actually only an expression of the reality that he has observed, in which different sentiments, attitudes and behaviours are often mixed up in this way. Fatalism is therefore attenuated by humour. The author also launches into social satire, the main targets of this being the Catholic Church and Francoism. This criticism of society is seen in the socio-cultural backwardness portrayed in some of the stories, and the ignorance of certain characters. The anticommunism of the regime is also treated in this way. Amusing anecdotes also offer the reader a commentary on morality by highlighting superstitions, beliefs or certain social behaviours, such as adultery or greed.

Nevertheless, despite this thematic continuity, the author's second book of stories is different to the first, because it is presented as an overarching chronicle of which the different stories form part, which gives it a greater unity of form. The title of the collection is the name of a fictional place in Moncada's Menquinensa and constitutes a kind of linking thread for the stories. In fact, the 'Cafè de la Granota' is where the narrator, who defines himself as a chronicler ('cronista'), meets up with old Cristòfol, who is present in most of the texts as a representative of the collective memory of the town, and as a secondary narrator. The narrator/chronicler is at pains to convince the reader that his story is the result of research and eye-witness reports. In general, he sees old Cristòfol as a reliable witness whenever he recounts an anecdote that forms part of the town's history, even though he has not necessarily lived through it directly himself. In effect, this character is just the transmitter of information that has been accumulated in popular memory over the years, mainly thanks to conversations in cafés, hence the title. The device of the second narrator, who confirms the authenticity of the facts that are recounted, is used throughout the book, which gives it its unity and consistence. It is one of the unifying elements for the texts, which — despite the variety of anecdotes presented — give it the illusion of being a single history: that of the former Mequinensa and its waterways.

These two first collections of stories were well received in the Catalan literary world, and some of the stories were quickly translated into Russian and Hungarian. These two translations are indicative of the literary value of these texts even though the author was only at the start of his publishing career. After 1993, the two books were translated into Spanish and published in Zaragoza, the capital of Aragón. The Aragonese press, and the

Spanish press in general, paid a lot of attention to these publications, publishing an important number of reviews.

Finally, we come to the third collection, *Calaveres atònites*, which was published fourteen years after the second. It forms part of the same continuum as far as the common setting for all the stories is concerned — the old town of Mequinensa — and this contributes to the creation of a common ambience. The author, as in his other works, brings the former Mequinensa back to life. These new stories are set at the beginning of the 1950s, at a time when the echoes of the Civil War had not yet been erased, and when no one was yet aware of the construction of the dam that would wipe out the town in 1971. Moncada reproduces the climate of the post-war years, the hardest part of the Franco regime, characterised by suspicion and the need for republicans and nationalists to live side by side despite having been on opposite sides during the Civil War. The book contains no dialogue — which signals an evolution from the two previous volumes where dialogue played an important role — and no description, but revolves around multiple voices, since each of the stories is presented in the form of a soliloquy. Each narrative focuses on a particular character who is given the right to speak. The short stories in the volume therefore have a common ingredient: orality. Apart from the four stories that have an epistolary form, they are all oral texts: their protagonists are people from Mequinensa who relate their problems aloud, whether to Crònides the judge, to his aunt Penèlope or to Mallol Fontcalda, a young lawyer from Barcelona who acts as the judge's secretary. More precisely, this makes the stories false monologues, since they are meant to be heard — or read, in the case of the letters — by another person. The stories are linked together by a single connecting thread, which means that they can be read as a whole, as a kind of episodic novel,[2] but also as a series of independent stories which all have Mequinensa as their common setting. In the Prologue, it is Mallol Fontcalda himself — as someone arriving in the town in the mid-fifties —

who leads the reader into the universe that constitutes the framework for all the stories. This means that the reader discovers the town through the gaze of an outsider — a gaze characterised by surprise since this was such a different world. In fact, the municipality even after the war was unanimously republican and left-wing, and very advanced socially considering the historical period and geographical space that surrounded it. The social climate there was progressive.

The explanation for the choice of the title of this third volume can be found in the last words of the prologue, at the end of which the narrator-character Mallol Fontcalda cites the words that the judge Crònides had said to him, by way of advice, the day after he arrived in Mequinensa. This phrase in which the curious title of the book appears, which will be discussed more fully later, allows us to affirm that the collection of stories opens with a philosophical reflection on the human condition and man's finite nature. Life is not just ephemeral, it is also insignificant. These stories incorporate a reflection on the passing of time and the brevity of life. Furthermore, the choice of the name of the character who forms the link between all the stories, Crònides the judge, is no accident, because it alludes to time (*chronos* in Greek). Despite this, a humorous tone predominates, since humour is present throughout the collection, which could be read as a comic treatment of Francoism. In fact, the parody of the moral discourse associated with National-Catholicism is one of the forms of irony in the stories, presenting a satirical vision of the clergy, since the Church is the main target of criticism. Irony is therefore especially directed at the moral and religious forces that dominated at that time, and also, of course, the forces of order. The most comical of these scenes are the ones which revolve around sex and the clergy.

This last volume marks an evolution in Moncada's satire on the Franco regime. In fact, in the first texts, the criticism is quite sparse and is achieved using small touches, while in the later stories it becomes a recurring topic and forms the main theme, organised around various lines of critique. Many of the texts have a light tone. Humour is also present in the titles of the stories, as well as in the words of many of the characters who respectfully address Crònides, following a kind of humorous protocol which becomes tangled to the point of confusion, giving the impression that the story will never actually begin. All of them want to shower him with flattery and use refined expressions mixed up with popular sayings appealing for good sense to prevail.

Moncada's Universe

Moncada's short stories have common themes and forms that make his personal style a particular one. Here, we will present the most obvious of these rather than giving a complete description.

Place

The most important common thread in the stories concerns space. Most of them are set within a referential space that is none other than the place of birth of the author, the former Mequinensa, in the geographical zone known as *la Franja de Ponent*, on the border between Catalonia and Aragón. Built at the confluence of the Ebro and the Segre, the town is connected to Catalan lands through its geography and its language, Catalan, even though administratively it depends on Aragón, forming part of the Province of Zaragoza. The centre of a mineral basin and heavy river traffic, the old town of Mequinensa, covered by the waters of a dam in 1971, constitutes, as has already been noted, the essential source of inspiration for the writer, as Isidor Cònsul has highlighted:

> Tota la seva obra s'ha orientat, pràcticament, a evocar el món perdut de l'antiga vila de Mequinensa, la seva ciutat nadiua, colgada sota les aigües d'un pantà. A la seva recuperació mítica ha dedicat els contes

> més significatius de *Històries de la mà esquerra* (1981) i de *El Cafè de la Granota* (1985), que es configuraven com peces desaparellades del retaule costumista de la vella Mequinensa. [...] Aquestes narracions, però, eren només les pinzellades prèvies del retaule definitiu, *Camí de sirga* (1988), la novel·la de Mequinensa, on el narrador ha sistematitzat tots els elements perduts del seu mite personalíssim [...].[3]
>
> (Practically all his work has revolved around the lost world of the old town of Mequinensa, the place of his birth, lost under the waters of a reservoir. The mythical recuperation of Mequinensa has been the objective of the most significant stories in *Històries de la mà esquerra* (1981) and *El Cafè de la Granota* (1985), which are configured as discreet pieces of a *costumbrista* portrait of the old Mequinensa. [...] However, these stories were just the preparatory sketches for the definitive portrait, *Camí de sirga* (1988), the novel of Mequinensa, in which the writer has systematized all the elements of this very personal myth [...].)

Forty-one of the forty-four published stories have the old town of Mequinensa as their geographical setting. Only three stories, which belong to the first volume, take place in another framework: 'Conte del vell tramviaire', 'Història de dies senars' and 'L'estremidora confessió de Joe Galàxia'. Actually, in the first two books the name of Mequinensa never directly appears in any story. In fact, the names used to refer to places are Llosa and Cantalaigua and, in most cases, the town is just referred to as 'la vila' or 'el poble'. Nevertheless, a relatively precise and coherent topography is fashioned from these first texts onwards. The author himself has stated that the places in his first stories refer to the Mequinensa of his childhood, and the later publication of the novels confirms this, since in these we find that in order to describe his own Mequinensa — which is explicitly named this time — he uses some of the same place names as in the first two collections of short stories. Thanks to this use of names and the places that are described in *Camí de sirga,* it is clear that the town in the first short stories is actually the same: that is, the Mequinensa created by Moncada.

This means that the action of the stories takes place essentially in Mequinensa, in its cafés, houses, streets or mines, or in nearby places, or by the river, and always in the town's past prior to 1970, the year in which the construction of the new town started, just before the dam itself was begun. The fictional Mequinensa, or the Mequinensa that has been recreated by Moncada, is a literary transfiguration of his own town. For this reason the toponyms are only partly mimetic, because the fictional place combines both real and imaginary names. Moncada's work brings together numerous toponyms from the town of his birth that exist alongside fictional names.[4] In the process of fictionalizing the real referential space, various distortions of reality are apparent, especially regarding the relationship between the toponyms used in fiction and those which belong to historical reality. Also, the author often invents places which never existed in the real Mequinensa but are organised according to a logic belonging to Moncada's own fiction, which results in the design of a fictional topography.

In this landscape belonging to the fictional Mequinensa, it is interesting to note the names of the businesses and the various establishments that are dotted throughout the work and contribute to the configuration of this urban space. Amongst the latter, apart from the many shops and workshops, we find numerous cafés whose names are mainly the result of literary creation. The presence of the cafés is a constant in Moncada's work, and is certainly not a result of chance as these particular places have been highlighted by the author. This is why the choice of title of the second collection of stories, *El Cafè de la Granota,* takes on an emblematic sense at the heart of his work as a whole. Moncada was conscious of the important role played by cafés in the transmission of collective memory in Mequinensa. He has even admitted that it was by frequenting these places that he was able to gather numerous anecdotes which inspired him when he came to write his own stories. The following are two of his declarations on this subject:

> Jo sóc un home de cafè, quan a Mequinensa encara es podia ser de cafè, però tot això ja ha desaparegut. Suposo que m'ha influït la manera de contar les històries que em trobava a les taules dels cafès.[5]
>
> (I'm a café-lover, at least when it was still possible to be a café-lover in Mequinensa, but all that has disappeared now. I suppose that I have been influenced by the way of telling stories that I encountered over the café tables.)

> Jo era un parroquià de cafè amb les orelles ben obertes unes vegades de manera deliberada i altres sense adonar-me'n. Moltes de les històries que explico en aquests llibres les he escoltades prenent un cafè.[6]
>
> (I was a regular attender in the cafés with my ears wide open, sometimes deliberately and sometimes without even realizing it. Many of the stories I tell in these books are things that I heard while having a coffee.)

It is interesting to observe, throughout his work, the social function carried out by the cafés where the townspeople express their various political opinions. The majority of people have progressive rather than conservative views, since the town was full of miners and workers and was essentially republican. This atmosphere predominates in the majority of the stories in the first two collections. In Moncada's various stories, each social group belongs to a particular café, which is often a place to express a particular political ideology. We see, for example, that the Cafè Central is frequented by republicans, the Cafè del Moll by socialists, the Cafè de la Muralla by communists. For its part, the Casino de la Roda is the café for the rich men of the town, as is the Casino dels Senyors.

If the writer has privileged the presence of the cafés at the heart of Mequinensa this is probably for two reasons: first, they represent a privileged space for the transmission of the collective memory, and also they are places for the expression of the town's political ideology, which is split between conservatives and progressives. This division is obvious throughout his work. The cafés also play an important role in the spatial configuration of the fictional Mequinensa and in the way the stories function diegetically, since this is essentially based on the process of anamnesis: numerous stories, that constitute the raw material for fiction, are transmitted in these cafés.

An Ironic Aesthetic

The study of the different components of the fictional world created by the author reveals the omnipresence of irony as a 'posture d'énonciation *construite en énoncé*' ('posture of enunciation *constructed as utterance*'), according to the definition given by Phillippe Hamon.[7] In other words, the irony does not spring from any particular phrase but corresponds to an attitude ('posture') that is constantly present. Moncada has chosen a global irony, a 'mode of discourse' in the sense attributed to this phrase by Beda Alleman: 'L'ironie littéraire, au sens exigeant de ce terme, ne peut jamais se limiter à l'ironie de phrases particulières' ('Literary irony, in the strict sense of the term, can never be limited to the irony of particular phrases').[8] The richness of Moncada's work is to a large extent linked to this ironic tone, and it is clear that this is one of the features that are detectable right from the first book of short stories. Nevertheless, this sense of humour is not just present in his books — in the treatment of certain themes, or in the names of people and places — but also in some of the articles that the writer published in the press, particularly 'Cabòries estivals'.[9] Irony also characterised his personal way of being and was a posture he adopted in the face of life. In one particular interview, Moncada defined himself in relation to his sense of irony, and compared himself — not without humour — to a famous character created by Valle Inclán, the Marquis of Bradomín:

> Como el personaje de Valle-Inclán, el marqués de Bradomín, pero, por supuesto, sin marquesado ni blasones; yo también nací feo, católico (en 1941, al menos en diciembre, cuando yo lo hice, se nacía así; en aquel mundo «feliz» hasta la genética se amoldaba

sumisamente a los decretos y a las encíclicas), más bien sentimental y, además, según parece, con un cierto sentido de la ironía, que suele acarrearme problemas «perfectamente serios», como diría don Antonio Machado. Exceptuando la anomalía biológica citada en segundo lugar, debo confesar que he sido incapaz, seguramente por desidia, de corregir estas (y otras muchas) imperfecciones.[10]

(Just like Valle-Inclán's character the Marquis of Bradomín, but, of course, without either a marquisate or crest, I was also born ugly, catholic (in 1941, at least in December as in my case, that's how people were born; in that 'happy' world even genetics bent themselves obediently to the decrees and encyclicals), somewhat sentimental and, besides, as it would appear, with a certain sense of irony, which tends to create 'perfectly serious' problems for me, as Antonio Machado would have said. Apart from the biological anomaly in second place on the list, I have to admit that I have been unable, no doubt through apathy, to correct these (and many other) imperfections.)

For Moncada, irony was just as much a part of his life as tragedy, as we can gather from his interview with Josep Gras:

Jesús Moncada narra en les seves novel·les uns fets tràgics, malauradament reals, que, malgrat els anys transcorreguts, continuen presents encara en la memòria de moltes persones. Però el seu estil narratiu, sense deixar de descriure les situacions dramàtiques que es viuen amb la necessària cruesa, no amaga un tel constant d'ironia que, en ocasions, reivindica obertament la seva presència en el text. L'escriptor mequinensà està convençut de la coexistència d'ambdues qualitats, tant en la literatura com en la pròpia vida; la vida és un tot i hi són tots els elements: tant els de la tragèdia com els de la comèdia, tots barrejats, l'únic que passa és que en un moment determinat els uns predominen sobre els altres.[11]

(Jesús Moncada narrates in his novels some tragic occurrences — real ones, unfortunately — that, despite the years that have passed, still continue to be present in the memories of many people. But his narrative style, although it does not shy away from describing with the necessary bluntness the dramatic situations that are experienced, cannot hide a constant layer of irony that, occasionally, openly demands a presence in the text. The

> Mequinensan writer is convinced of the coexistence of both qualities, in literature and in life itself; life is a totality and all elements are there, whether tragic or comic, all mixed up, and the only thing that happens is that at a given moment some predominate over others.)

Moncada's perception of irony as being a key element of life identifies his conception of it with what Beda Alleman calls 'l'ironie nue et constructive de l'état du monde' ('naked irony that is constructive of the state of the world'), meaning irony 'donnée par avance dans les rapports qu'ont les choses entre elles' ('given in advance in the relationships that things have between themselves'), that literary irony understood as a mode of discourse simply reflects.[12]

It is this enunciative position that predominates in the texts of an author who has also sometimes defined his gaze as a mirror held up to reality, which is how he maintains a sense of distance:

> El Jesús Moncada escriptor procura ser només un mirall de tot el que està passant. Se'n distancia, perquè, si no, aleshores, la ironia que sura a tots els meus llibres desapareixeria, i a mi em sembla que aquesta ironia i aquest humor són necessaris.[13]
>
> (Jesús Moncada the writer tries to be nothing more than a mirror of everything that is happening. He distances himself from it, because otherwise the irony that thrives in all my books would disappear, and it seems to me that this irony and humour is necessary.)

This declaration allows us to understand his conception of writing and the role of the writer. However, humour is present to a greater or lesser extent depending on the plot of his stories, as he himself stated on the occasion of the publication of his third collection:

> J.B. — I l'humor? Ja era planificat o hi heu arribat espontàniament, inevitablement?

J.M. — No planifico mai. Forma part de la meva manera de veure les coses. Que aquest humor suri més o menys, depèn de l'argument de la història. A *Estremida memòria* hi havia humor, però contingut, pel caràcter tràgic de la història. En aquest cas l'humor ho amera tot.[14]

(J.B. — And the humour? Was that already planned or did it come spontaneously, inevitably?

J.M. — I never plan. It's part of my way of seeing things. Whether the humour surfaces a lot or a little depends on the plot of the story. There was humour in *Estremida memòria* but it was contained, because of the tragic nature of the story. In this case everything is drenched in humour.)

Humour allows us to observe reality while distancing ourselves from it, but this distance means, for Moncada, another way of seeing it. Jankélévitch speaks of this same need for perspective when he describes irony as 'ce recul et ce minimum d'oisiveté sans lesquels il n'y a pas de représentation possible: l'esprit se décolle de la vie [...], l'ironie introduit dans notre savoir le relief et l'échelonnement de la perspective' ('that distance and degree of inactivity without which no representation is possible: the mind becomes detached from life [...], irony introduces into our knowledge the depth and spread of perspective').[15] This distance from the real is indispensable for a more accurate and contrasted perception of reality, which according to Moncada is always double since it oscillates between tragedy and comedy. Critics have considered the humour-drama dialectic in Moncada's writing to be a great discovery, particularly when it comes to the evocation of the lost world of Mequinensa, since this might have given rise to an elegiac and nostalgic tone which, in fact, has been avoided through the recourse to irony:

En aquest món que Moncada basteix era fàcil lliurar-se a l'enyorament o al cant de la melangia més ostentosa i rondinaire. L'autor ha tingut prou tacte per salvar l'escull que representava aquest enyorament, sens dubte element present en tota l'obra. En canvi, aquest element es manté cautament per sota de l'humor i la ironia, a vegades, i del to dramàtic d'altres. La dialèctica humor-drama implica certa força narrativa i dissenya un corpus soterrat de costums i vivències atàviques.

(Moncada's universe could easily succumb to nostalgia or overblown and carping melancholy. However, he manages to avoid the trap of such nostalgia, which does undoubtedly run through his work, and use it instead to underpin both the humour and irony of his texts and their drama. The tension between humour and drama informs his narrative and helps fashion an alternative body of traditions and centuries-old experiences.)[16]

For the writer, the various forms of humour allow him to relativise the reflection imposed by writing and to see all the different nuances.[17] Sometimes this humour is macabre and harsh, but at other times it is full of tenderness and comprehension towards the victims and protagonists of comic situations, which reveals the sympathy the author feels for them. In some stories, the humour comes from anecdote, looking at the absurd or shocking side of a situation. Sometimes the comedy has a didactic character, as it used to have in the satires and moralising fables of the ancient world. At other times, the humour is incisive and serves to denounce and ridicule questionable moral attitudes, offering a lively critique of society under Francoism. Thus, using a fine irony and situations that verge on the absurd, the narrator reflects the pettiness and stinginess of the characters, or the hypocrisy and sexual repression of the upper classes which, in 'Amor fatal en decúbit supí' ('Fatal Love in the Supine Position'),[18] for example, give rise to much hilarity.

Football as a social phenomenon, and the infantile or amusing reactions of its fans, are the subject of several stories, such as 'Un enigma i set tricornis' ('A Puzzle and Seven Tricorns').[19] Shots at goal, falls and mistakes that make the reader laugh also appear as humoristic elements. The exaggerated innocence or ignorance of certain characters is also a source of amusement for the reader (as in the case of 'Senyora Mort, carta de Miquel Garrigues').[20]

Humour certainly allows tensions to be reduced and the numerous criticisms present in the short stories — such as those of the Franco regime and the Church — to be softened, but also sometimes helps to lessen the drama of pain or anger.

The Characters

The third constant of Moncada's stories concerns their protagonists, who are of course invented but are always inspired by the inhabitants of Mequinensa, especially the witnesses to the town's disappearance. In the three collections it is the boatmen and the miners who predominate, and they always and without exception express themselves in their local language, most often colloquially. Moncada was friends with sailors and boat-builders, and had the opportunity to talk with them about their profession, which inspired him when he came to creating the sailors in his stories.

This means that, throughout the stories, the characterisation of the protagonists is essentially situated between reality and fiction, and is very often linked to the lived experience of the writer. Sometimes his protagonists are inspired by real people whose identity he has hidden. For example, some of the nicknames that he uses really existed in Mequinensa.[21] This is most notably the case with the nickname of the star who sang at the *Cafè del Jardí* in Mequinensa at the start of the twentieth century, Paca la Xina, who becomes 'the cuplé singer' of the story 'D'uns vells papers de música' ('Old Sheet Music'),[22] and is inspired by a real woman from Mequinensa, who had the same nickname because of her oriental appearance. In the work, other characters directly inspired by reality keep their name or nickname in fiction.[23]

The reader comes across many of these names more than once in the stories and novels. The reuse of the same names contributes to the unity of Moncada's work, since the faithful reader has the impression that all the stories echo one another. The same figures reappear in several stories that have a similar setting, which favours the existence of a continuity in his work and gives the reader the impression of an established world.[24] Each story seems to be just a partial, anecdotic vision of a more complex world. This means that the different stories give rise to various family lines, respecting the temporal logic and functions attributed to each one of them.

The character who is present throughout Moncada's work, and whose characterisation and lineage are undoubtedly the most precise, is Honorat del Rom. He was created in the first collections as 'Honorat the Apothecary'.[25] However, it is in the novel *Camí de sirga* that the writer constructs for him a past that includes a great-grandfather who killed one of Napoleon's soldiers during the War of Independence;[26] Honorat del Rom succeeds his father Honorat del Café as the apothecary in their pharmacy.[27] We meet Honorat del Rom again in the last collection of stories,[28] in which he is characterised in exactly the same way as the previous ones, as an atheist republican who is interested as much in politics as in entertainment, who eschews formality, and who is also one of the rare individuals who has studied and has some interest in culture, as Emili Bayo points out.[29]

In this way, despite the temporal distance that separates the writing of each book and the multitude of figures that people Moncada's fiction, this world is characterised by its coherence. The literary universe, unique to this writer, that Hèctor Moret has described as a 'microcosm',[30] in which collective memory plays the main role, is a world based on reality but which becomes mythical thanks to Moncada's pen. The fact remains that this results from an artistic construction born both from a creative enthusiasm and from the work of the novelist's gaze, which is normally translated into an ironic distancing from reality. This often gives rise to texts that are imbued with a great tenderness towards the characters, since — as he himself affirms — Moncada loved the people he created:

> La teva narrativa està amarada de tendresa. A «L'ull esquerre de Tomàs d'Atura», Tastaboires, parlant dels vilatans, diu: «Mirate'ls, Adolorida... Porten les butxaques plenes d'il·lusions cobertes de teranyines, d'esperances secretes, de pors i de cendres. El fàstic, però, és el que més abunda. I la por.» Em sembla que en aquest i en d'altres paràgrafs poses de manifest el que sents envers la condició humana i de retruc envers els personatges. És així?
>
> [...] Pel que fa als personatges, no puc negar que acabo estimant-me'ls.[31]
>
> ('Your narrative is full of tenderness. In "L'ull esquerre de Tomàs d'Atura" ("Tomàs d'Atura's Left Eye"), Tastaboires, talking about the townspeople, says "Look at them, Adolorida... Their pockets are full of cobweb-covered illusions, secret hopes, fears and ashes. But the most abundant thing is disgust. And fear." It seems to me that in this and other paragraphs you reveal what you feel about the human condition and, at the same time, about the characters. Is that right?'
>
> 'As far as the characters are concerned, I can't deny that I end up loving them.')

This sympathy is mainly expressed in the humour that results from the innocence and simplicity of the protagonists, who are treated tenderly, especially when they are humble people. This means that the most successful characters are the naïve or innocent individuals such as old Atanasi in 'Conte del vell tramviaire'.[32] The tram driver experiences a feeling of despair when he reaches retirement age and has to leave his job and the tram, since he is very attached to the vehicle.

In the last collection, *Calaveres atònites,* there are three main characters: the judge Crònides Valldabó, Mallol Fontcalda — a young lawyer from Barcelona who comes to Mequinensa to take up the position as secretary to the judge —, and Penèlope Valldabó, the judge's aunt. However, the writer also brings back some of the characters from his previous works, such as Arnau de Roda or Honorat del Rom, through whom we hear the voice of conversations held in cafés and therefore the memory of the town. As we turn the pages, the reader sees a procession of characters who combine to create comic situations: several bigots, pious women, a prostitute with an enlightened mind, the prurient priest, the cardinal, the governor's wife, the pharmacist, the Civil Guard sergeant, the barge owner, the postman…

The choice of Crònides as the first name of the judge who forms the link between all the stories in this collection merits some attention: in fact, it is not neutral, as it alludes to time (*chronos* in Greek). Even though humour is omnipresent in the book, these stories should not be considered banal, as they incorporate a reflection on the passing of time and the brevity of life. It is precisely Crònides himself who expresses, in the last words of the prologue,[33] a philosophical reflection on the human condition and the finite nature of man, and it is on this note that the stories begin:

> No treballi tant, senyor secretari, deixi la paperassa i vingui a finestrejar. Guaiti, fixi's en aqueixa noia tan bonica que travessa la plaça. No badi, cregui'm, això dura poc. En un tres i no res, passem d'embrions incerts a calaveres atònites.[34]
>
> (Don't work so hard, Mr Secretary, leave the paperwork and come and have a look out of the window. Here, look at that pretty girl crossing the square. Don't stand there gaping, believe me, this doesn't last very long. Before we know it we've gone from uncertain embryos to astonished skulls.)

Life is not just fleeting but also insignificant. It is a short journey, so we must make the most of it. Crònides' words therefore echo the classical motif of *carpe diem*, but, at the same time, the vision of death expressed here seems to have its roots in the existential pessimism of the baroque regarding the brevity of life: to live is already to die a little. As a result, the choice of the judge's first name is not insignificant, especially since in his ambivalent conception of time we see the two sides of the treatment of the theme of death in all of Moncada's writing, as Isidor Cònsul says:

> A mi em sembla que la intenció general de Jesús Moncada va en aquest doble sentit: una disposició vital per viure cada instant

> amb joiosa intensitat i un cert escarni de la mort, vista com un tot que ens acompanya i que hem de procurar no prendre'ns gaire seriosament. Una actitud que lliga la vitalitat de l'instant a la ironia i l'escepticisme davant d'una existència massa breu i incerta.[35]

> (It seems to me that the general intention of Jesús Moncada has the following double sense: a fundamental willingness to live each moment with joyous intensity and a certain mocking of death, which is seen as a totality that accompanies us but that we should try not to take too seriously. An attitude that links the vitality of the moment to irony and scepticism regarding an existence which is all too brief and uncertain.)

The name Crònides therefore has a double function: on one hand it allows the philosophical inclinations of the character to be portrayed, and other the other it gives us a key for interpreting the texts by the author that deal with the theme of time. Chrònides does not have the features of a symbolic character, and can be better seen as representing the voice of the writer, who expresses through him his concept of life. Besides, this judge, who is described as tolerant and liberal, seems to embody different facets of the man who was Jesús Moncada, even though Moncada himself declared that there was nothing of himself in this character.[36] Through his function as a judge he represents the ideal of justice held by the author who, according to his sister, was a staunch defender of human rights.[37] As for Chrònides' concept of life, this too is similar to Moncada's own: he is first and foremost an epicurean, who likes to take full advantage of life, but Chrònides is also, like Moncada, an agnostic pessimist, as is shown by one of his phrases that the author chose to use as an epigraph for the collection: 'Here, Mr Secretary, the only believable eternity at our disposal is daily life'.[38] This reflection, from a character who is getting on in years, could have been a phrase spoken by Jesús Moncada, since at the time he was drafting his last collection of stories at the end of the 1990s he was in his fifties himself. Furthermore, when I met him in July 1997, I asked him about his pessimism, and his response, which confirms his crude realism and his agnosticism, was the following: 'Pessimista, no. Jo penso que les coses sempre acaben de la mateixa manera, és a dir a nivell individual, acaben amb la mort, i punt. I això és prou «fotut»!' ('Not a pessimist, no. I think that things always turn out in the same way, I mean, on an individual level, they end in death, and that's it. And that's a bit of a bugger!')

There are other reflections of the writer in his work on different levels, in particular, in characters that share his passion for painting, one of the main aspects of his identity. From the first collections of stories, Moncada regularly creates protagonists who are painters. In one of his articles, the author compares himself to one of them he created for the story 'Història de dies senars' from *Històries de la mà esquerra:* '[...] guanyar-me la vida, com el protagonista d'un dels meus contes pintant en sèrie batalles navals, postes de sol i paisatges amb cérvols' ('[...] to earn a living, like one of the protagonists of my stories mass-producing paintings of naval battles, sunsets and landscapes full of deer').[39] The novelist has occasionally responded positively to the question of whether this fictional painter had something to do with his own experiences.[40] In this case there is certainly a reflection of his role as a commercial painter. The story begins with an autobiographical passage in which the homodiegetic author is none other than the fictional painter himself.

> En aquell temps jo compartia les golfes d'una casa del carrer de Girona amb un gat que es deia Caius. Em trobava sense feina i per viure pintava en sèrie batalles navals, postes de sol i paisatges amb cérvols, pels quals em donaven una misèria. Tot just per mal menjar i pair pitjor.
> De nit escrivia històries de gent senzilla i parlava amb el gat. Caius era un felí de fumeral, un pòtol voltateulades avesat a viure al dia i a esquivar el cop de pedra. Això l'havia fet molt comprensiu i es passava hores escoltant les meves cabòries.

>   -Ja veuràs, Caius. Un dia tothom llegirà les meves històries.[41]
>
>   (At that time I lived in the attic of a house in Girona Street with a cat called Caius. I was out of work and to earn a living I mass-produced paintings of naval battles, sunsets and landscapes full of deer, that I was paid a pittance for. Just enough to scrape by.
>
>   At night I wrote stories about humble people and talked to the cat. Caius was a chimney cat, a roof-top vagrant who would go out during the day and dodge the stones that were thrown in his direction. That had made him very understanding and he spent hours listening to my troubles.
>
>   'You'll see, Caius, one day everyone'll read my stories'.)

Here, a form of literary transfiguration is performed on the place, since Moncada also lived in an attic, but in the district of Gràcia, in Camprodon Street. As for the writer's pet, for many years this was actually a dog, and not a cat as in the story. Furthermore, another analogy connects character and author: he also wrote stories in the semi-darkness in the hope that one day they would be read. Another detail of the story points to another resemblance: the narrator/painter describes his commercial paintings as 'rubbish'.[42] Moncada was also no fan of these banal tableaux that were made to sell and were not real works of art in the sense that he would understand it.

Many teasing reflections of the personality of the writer in the figures of the fictional characters can be seen in Moncada's work. Nevertheless, self-writing does not just operate through the identification with individual protagonists, but also through the sympathy with the collective cast which assumes a great importance in this fictional world, especially since Moncada considered himself to be a part of it and felt a sense of solidarity with the inhabitants of Mequinensa, experiencing the same emotions about the events that affected them, which are reconstructed through the collective memory that is also part of his own heritage.

The Voice of the People

The writer from *La Franja,* who was a great lover of the Catalan language — as is demonstrated by the great lexical richness and precision of his expression — manages to bring it to life by exploring the possibilities of oral language, which originates outside literary language. The issue at the heart of his writing is to re-appropriate 'la parole vive' ('the living word') which Paul Zumthor speaks about,[43] by reproducing the oral model that belongs to popular language — a familiar register, typical aspects of oral language, the vocabulary related to life on the river as it was heard in Mequinensa, etc. — but also by introducing some of the discursive genres that come from oral literature.

Putting into narrative an oral discourse that belongs to popular memory raises the question of the links between writing and orality, by which I mean the ways in which the voice can be inserted into written literary texts. Moncada's fiction is peppered with various indications of orality, which are incorporated into the writing in a very natural way since they appear in passages of oral communication such as dialogue or monologue. However, sometimes the narration itself is affected by features that are characteristic of oral discourse.

Dialogue is very much a feature of the short stories, and this introduces the illusion of orality. The numerous changes of speaker either take the form of dialogue in its true sense, or monologue. This is how the voice of the characters emerges, as they separate themselves from narrative mediation in order to present themselves directly, either in fragments of dialogue that are inserted into the narrative or in monologues. The short stories are therefore in many ways a transcription of oral language. This slippage of the written towards the oral is a way of giving value to the living word. Moncada's dialogues contribute to the creation of an illusion of referentiality by imitating, without limits, oral language in all its registers, which the characters use depending on their origins or the context in which they evolve. Through the use of idiolects or sociolects, they mark out a clear difference between the discourse of the narrator and that of the characters, which reinforces the mimetic effect.

Direct discourse can be signified in various ways in Moncada's work. The presence of dialogue in the first two volumes of stories is principally signified by the traditional use of a carriage return with a dash, and a greater or lesser proportion of verbs of speaking. As a result of his concern to reflect reality, Moncada's dialogue in all its forms reproduces numerous turns of phrase borrowed from oral language. He reflects its characteristic traits, such as unfinished phrases, sudden changes of topic, frequent use of exclamations to express surprise, disagreement, impatience ('Vinga! — 'Come on!') and other feelings ('Déu n'hi do!' — 'Goodness me!'), the presence of onomatopoeia ('patapaf!'), and linguistic padding ('Redéu!' — 'blimey!'; 'què cony...' — 'what the hell...'); there are also markers that express spontaneity with a word that might sometimes be rude depending on context ('Hòstia,[44] noi' — 'bloody hell, boy!'), swearwords ('Dimoni!'; 'bloody hell!', 'Que diguin missa!' — 'They can get stuffed!') or terms of abuse ('Guaita que arribes a ser cap de soca!' — 'be careful, you're turning into a blockhead!';[45] 'Porca' — 'bitch!').

The living word is also reproduced through the use of a familiar register or even slang.[46] The level of language chosen is always appropriate to the person who is speaking, which obviously contributes to its realism. Some examples of this include the phrases:

> — La ballarem — sembla que remugà Joanot de Monegre, lacònic, eixut i depressiu com sempre.[47] ('We'll be in a pickle', ruminated Joanot de Monegre, as laconic, dry and depressive as ever.)
> and
> — Et farem empassar el xiulet! — rugia la tripulació del llaüt Soledat [...].[48]

('We'll make you swallow your whistle', roared the crew of the barge Soledat.)

The passages of dialogue also imitate the stylistics of popular language. Sometimes the order of the phrase is modified: the characters omit the noun or the verb, or a whole part of the phrase might just be suggested ('És que...' — 'The thing is...').[49] Hyperbole or euphemism ('com que no saps mai què pot passar en un país tan perfecte con aquest' — 'since you never know what might happen in a perfect country like ours')[50] are some of the other features of oral style that pepper the dialogues or monologues. The oral model also comes through in the stereotypes of oral language that are found throughout both the dialogue and the narration. In fact, the author uses a large quantity of ready-made expressions, of many different kinds, without restricting himself to localisms.

The geographical origin of the writer might lead us to believe that this choice of orality necessarily means using the dialect of his native town, since this is the referent of his work. Moncada certainly demonstrated his attachment to his native language, meaning the Catalan that was spoken in Mequinensa before it was flooded. His passion for words has led him to recuperate some items of vocabulary and revive them thanks to his characters' spontaneity, and dialectal forms are not excluded from this. Nevertheless, it was never a question of acting as an archaeologist, or linguist. His literary language is therefore not a narrow reflection of the spoken language used in Mequinensa — there is no dialectalisation, despite the orality which radiates from his stories. The author himself affirmed that his characters did not exclusively use local varieties, because he thought that this would be a dangerous thing to do in literature.[51] This is why his writing obviously contains certain specific traits of the North-Western dialect, but Eastern forms are not excluded. However, as Mercè Biosca has shown,[52] the recourse to the North-Western variety is more frequent on a lexical level than morphosyntactically.[53]

His excellent knowledge of the Catalan language and its dialectal nuances explains the great lexical richness of his books. The writer's language is the product of a real literary act of will, since he has made his linguistic choices based on their narrative effectiveness, avoiding the traps both of the standard language and of an excess of localism.

Relating this to the topic of set expressions,[54] we see that, as a consequence, expressions of a strictly local character (i.e. from the Catalan-speaking zone of the *Franja de Ponent*) rub shoulders with others that belong to Western or Eastern Catalan. Amongst the typical features of oral language, the characters also use proverbs, although less than other types of expressions.[55] It is certainly the case that the reproduction of this kind of orality, with its different elements, heightens the realistic effect by bringing verisimilitude to the narrative discourse, but at the same time it inscribes the literary text in the tradition of oral language, taking into account that the latter encompasses all dimensions of this linguistic reality.

Direct speech — whether it takes the form of dialogue or monologue — is not the only space invested with a living language that often also affects the narration. The reference to orality is also visible especially when the narrator reuses in transposed discourse — either indirect or free indirect speech — not only a lexis that belongs to orality but also the familiar register of language that is differentiated depending on each character, bringing a great dynamism to the literary discourse.

The oral model manifests itself in the narration in the same way as in the dialogues and monologues. Linguistic stereotypes, which the author uses abundantly, are found throughout the stories, as well as certain turns of phrase characteristic of oral language which relate, for example, to the placement of words in the phrase, or to the insertion of clauses. Some of the syntactic traits stem from the typical features of oral literatures, and stylistic invariants such as parataxis, a characteristic structure of conversational syntax.

It is not only the language of orality but the narrative activity of collective memory itself that the fiction tries to mimic by introducing discursive forms that belong to the oral tradition that nourishes Moncada's stories, inscribing in the texts both the spontaneous oral productions of the people and the forms belonging to oral literature. The writer uses a rich variety of resources to construct this oral material and bring together orality and literary discourse, taking up the challenge of stepping from folklore to literature. The popular voice takes on many oral activities with varying forms: rumours and superstitions, legends and histories, etc.

In most cases, orality is the act of the voices of the town who tell stories ('històries', 'contalles') in a particular social context of 'tertúlies', whether these take place in the street or — more often — in cafés, which are the places where the most unlikely tales are passed on, as are the legends. Critics have underlined the fact that Moncada plays with the mechanisms of this type of story that are passed on in the town's cafés:

> Moncada juga, a més a més, amb els mecanismes del *racconto* popular, de café. Està convençut que el café és la Universitat més activa per la majoria, el lloc on creixen i s'ensorren fames i prestigis, l'aula oberta a tota mena de debats.
>
> [...] Moncada s'ha destacat com un autor que creu en els valors de la tradició oral, estructura bàsica sobre la qual sustenta les seves narracions.[56]
>
> (Moncada also plays with the mechanisms of popular storytelling as it occurs in the cafés. He is convinced that for most people the café is their main form of University, the place where fame and prestige grow and fade, the classroom open to all kinds of debates.
>
> [...] Moncada stands out as an author who believes in the values of oral tradition, the basic structure upon which his stories are constructed.)

Rumour is one of the products of oral activity which regularly nourishes Moncada's fiction:

> Des de l'amagatall de la finestra, la xafarderia mesurava dolors, indiferències, mesquineses i luxes per a futures murmuracions.[57]
> (Hiding at the window, the gossips weighed up pain, indifference, meanness and luxuries for future whispers.)

Rumour often becomes part of the plot through the various narrators, and the reader finds many allusions to these disparaging comments that return again and again, as in the story 'Els delfins' ('The Dauphins') which tackles the unpredictable side of the rumours spread by the collective voice, often with malicious interpretations:

> [...] quan donava el condol a les dones sense atorrollar-me, d'una manera sentida encara que un pèl distant, a fi d'evitar interpretacions malicioses a càrrec de la xafarderia vilatana. Les dones són material delicat i trencadís, i cal parar-hi molt compte. A més, tothom és sempre tan pendent de mi que qualsevol gest dubtós, qualsevol paraula més enllà d'una altra podrien provocar un desastre: quan la bola de la murmuració comença a rodar, malament rai; no saps mai què en resultarà. I, avui, encara havia de tenir més cura que els altres dies. Un diumenge, fa quaranta-cinc anys, la Carme, ara vídua del Constantí, va ballar amb mi tres vegades seguides; la vila té la memòria llarga i no volia que hi hagués de què parlar si em mostrava més afectuós del que pertocava. Això no obstant, suposo que tot déu s'haurà adonat, en reparar el meu capteniment digne i sever, que d'aquella foguera no queda ni la cendra, almenys per la meva banda.[58]
> ([...] while I was expressing my sympathy to the ladies, without going too far, in a genuine but somewhat distant manner, so as to avoid malicious interpretations from the towns' gossips. Women are made of delicate and fragile material, and this must be properly taken into account. Besides, everyone is always watching me so closely that any doubtful gesture, any word that comes after another, could cause a disaster: when the ball of rumour starts to roll, watch out — you never know what the result will be. And today I had to be even more careful than other

days. One Sunday, forty-five years ago, Carme, now Constantí's widow, danced with me three times in a row; the town has a long memory and I didn't want to give them anything to talk about if I came across as more affectionate to her than was appropriate. Despite this, I suppose that anybody could have seen, from my dignified and severe comportment, that there remained not even a trace of ash from that particular bonfire, at least on my part.)

These many slanderous or untruthful rumours that are circulated by the inhabitants of Mequinensa about other members of the community, are found throughout Moncada's short stories and make an important contribution to their plot.

Superstitions can also be considered as a type of oral discourse which serves as a vehicle for collective memory. In the story 'Guardeu-vos de somiar genives esdentegades' ('Beware of dreaming about toothless gums'),[59] the character of Adelaida believes in a series of superstitions, especially the one that gives the story its title. In order to ward off the bad luck that is prefigured by the nightmare in which she loses her teeth (which, according to popular belief, presages the death of a loved one), she takes ever more elaborate precautions in her daily routine so as to avoid the accumulation of misfortune, and lights a small candle in front of the image of the town's patron saint to protect her family from misadventure, especially her grandson Carles:

> Damunt el marbre de la calaixera, als peus de la imatge de guix pintat de la patrona de la vila, l'animeta, immòbil sobre l'oli del vas, feia una claror daurada. L'Adelaida l'havia encès al matí, a fi que les notícies de Lleida fossin bones. També, al llarg del dia, havia parat molt compte a no llençar la sal, ni trencar l'olier, o deixar les tisores obertes, amb mires d'allunyar la malastruga; tanmateix, tot i aquestes precaucions, no se sentia tranquil·la. No es podia treure del pensament el malson que havia tingut tres nits abans: havia somiat que li queien els queixals; s'havia vist esdentegada, amb les genives sangonoses. I allò — era cosa sabuda — significava que la mort planava sobre la família. Angoixada,

s'encaboriava amb el nét, no es podia estar de pensar que aquell signe esgarrifós era la premonició d'un esdeveniment terrible. I encara que la consogra sempre insistia que allò eren bestieses, animalades sense solta ni volta, no aconseguia desencaparrar-la. ¿Qui gosaria negar que la Júlia Borges havia emmalaltit d'un mal lleig després de trobar set vegades set ametlles a l'ampit de la finestra, i havia anat a parar al fossar al cap de quatre dies? ¿Com havia aconseguit, l'Antònia Vinyes, que la pestilència invisible que li matava les gallines s'allunyés de casa seva, sinó espargint sal, mentre repetia tres vegades un encanteri — «qui em vulgui mal es fongui com aquesta sal» — a la llinda de la porta?[60]

(On the marble top of the chest of drawers, at the feet of the painted plaster image of the patron saint of the town, the wick, immobile on top of the oil in the container, gave a golden light. Adelaida had lit it that morning, so that the news she expected from Lledia would be good. As the day went on, she was also very careful not to spill salt, or break the oil jar, or leave the scissors open, so as to ward off back luck; but despite all these precautions she did not feel happy. She could not get out of her mind the bad dream she had had three nights before: she had dreamt that her molars fell out, and had seen herself toothless, with bleeding gums. And that — as everyone knew — meant that death was hanging over the family. She worried anxiously about her grandson, and could not help thinking of that horrifying sign as the premonition of a terrible occurrence. And even though her daughter's mother-in-law always insisted that all that was rubbish, foolishness without rhyme or reason, she could not get it out of her head. Who would dare to deny that Júlia Borges had fallen ill with a terrible illness after seven times finding seven almonds on the parapet of the window and had ended up in the graveyard just four days later? How had Antònia Vinyes managed to get the terrible plague that killed her chickens to leave her house, except by scattering salt and repeating a charm — 'whoever wishes me ill, may he dissolve like this salt will' — three times under the door lintel?)

These popular beliefs that give rise to superstitious behaviours on the part of the characters appear at various points in the work.

Superstitions linked to death appear especially in the stories contained in the early collections, such as 'Traducció del llatí'

('Latin Translation'), in which the omniscient narrator gives voice to a popular belief that the dead can create trouble if their wishes regarding being laid to rest are not respected:

> El vell Atanasi va eixir d'entre la gent i es va plantar al mig del camí, vora la caixa.
> — Que em pengin si no té tota la raó! — havia cridat, alhora que brandia amb fúria la gaiata —. L'enterrarem com cal!
> Un murmuri aprovatori es va estendre per la comitiva. Calia que el difunt fos aplacat — ofici de capellans fins aleshores —, que les seves despulles trobessin la pau abans de donar-li terra. Perquè l'alè d'un mort posseït per l'odi podia fer malbé les collites, podrir les aigües i escampar arreu del poble, el mateix que un mal aire, les llavors empestades de totes les maleses.[61]
>
> (Old Atanasi came out from the mass of people and stood right in the middle of the road, near the coffin.
> "Strike me down if I'm not right!" he had yelled, furiously brandishing his crook. "We're going to bury him properly!"
> An approving murmur rippled through the funeral procession. The deceased must be placated — which up until now had been the priests' job — and his remains must find peace before being consigned to the earth. Because the breath of a dead person possessed by hatred could ruin harvests, turn water stagnant and, just like an ill wind, could spread through the town the rotten seeds of all manner of ills.)

In addition to these forms of the popular voice, which have a strong presence throughout the work, other forms borrowed from oral literature also become a source that can be reworked in writing. The many voices that belong to the collective of Mequinensa contribute a diverse range of stories that configure Moncada's fiction. It is worth noting that the term 'històries' — (hi)stories — was chosen by the writer to describe the texts in his first collection, *Històries de la mà esquerra*. These stories are part of the way of life of the inhabitants of Mequinensa, which is why Moncada has one of the fictional characters of *Calaveres atònites* say:

> I comprenc l'interès de la gent, aquestes històries fan greix, ajuden a viure [...] Si jo mateix xalo amb les històries dels altres, he d'acceptar que els altres xalin amb les meves [...].[62]
> (And I understand why people are interested, these stories are enjoyable, they make life worth living. [...] If I get pleasure out of other people's stories, I have to accept that they will get pleasure out of mine.)

The different stories that reach the town's inhabitants give the community a certain pleasure and constitute a form of social relations that are made explicit in Moncada's work. He has in any case observed repeatedly that 'qualsevol nucli humà és una font inexhaurible d'històries' ('any human nucleus is an inexhaustible source of stories')[63] and that 'qualsevol col·lectivitat humana és un niu d'històries' ('any human collective is a breeding ground for stories').[64]

These oral stories are often also described as 'contalles', meaning tales or fables, like the one that occurs in the short story 'Riada' ('Flood'), which tells of the voyage of a barge during a significant flooding event on the Ebro river, something that could have ended in tragedy:

> Del maleït viatge en van fer moltes contalles per tota la ribera: que si el Sant Crist havia canviat de color, que si va desclavar una mà, que si els regalims de sang se li van allargar per les galtes... Històries que escampen pels cafès, tota la culpa de les quals la té el Moles, que es morirà embafadet de veritats perquè no conta més que mentides. Però, de tota manera, no m'hauria estranyat mica que al de la creu li hagués passat tot això que conten i molt més, perquè allò del pedret va ser terrible. Encara veig el vell Gòdia, mentre el Moles udolava que ens matàvem, donar un cop de timó cap a la dreta i repenjar-se sobre l'arjau amb mig cos fora la borda. Van cruixir totes les juntes del llaüt, però el vell, que encara no he pogut aclarir d'on va treure tanta força, va adreçar la nau i vam passar, el mateix que un llamp, a quatre dits del roquissar. Vam estar a punt d'esbocinar-nos. Per això dic que ben bé li hauria pogut canviar el color al Crist! Ara, que va ser ell, el Crist, qui va cridar «Timó a la dreta, Gòdia, que ens la fotem!»,

mentida podrida! El vell Gòdia podia ser més tossut que una mula, però no calia que ningú li digués el que havia de fer, que, de feines de riu, en sabia més que Déu.[65]

(Many tales about that fated voyage were heard up and down the river's edge: that the Christ had changed colour, that one of its hands became unnailed, that trickles of blood ran down its cheeks... Stories that spread through the cafés, the blame for which can be laid squarely at the feet of Moles, who when he dies will still be carrying a surfeit of truths since he only ever tells lies. But, in any case, I wouldn't have been surprised if all this had happened to the chap on the cross and more besides, because those rocks were terrible. I can still see old Godia, as Moles howled that they were going to die, turning the wheel to the right and finding himself hanging over the tiller with half his body overboard. All the barge's joints creaked, but the old man (and I still haven't worked out how he managed to find so much strength) managed to put the boat back on course, and like a bolt of lightning we shot past the rocky outcrop just a couple of inches away. We had been about to be torn to shreds. That's why I say that the Christ might well have changed colour! On the other hand, the idea that it was him, the Christ, who shouted 'Hard right, Gòdia, we're in deep trouble', is a dirty rotten lie. Old Gòdia might be as stubborn as a mule but no one needed to tell him what to do. When it came to working on the river, he knew more than God.)

In this story it is clear that the narrator, a character who actually participated in the adventure he is recounting, gives his version of events as a direct witness, but at the same time he refutes others' versions ('mentida podrida'). The first phrase of the extract given above is a hyperbole ('Del maleït viatge en van fer moltes contalles per tota la ribera'): one on hand, this brings more realism to the story by highlighting the great interest it arouses, which can be explained by its extraordinary aspects; on the other hand, this is one of the characteristic recourses of such oral stories, where exaggeration is used in order to attract the attention and curiosity of the listener.

In oral stories that are transmitted through the collective memory of a community there is a permanent tension between truth and lies, reality and imagination. We see this dialectic in some of the stories, especially in *Calaveres atònites* where old Pòlit stands by the truth of his version of the story of Hannibal, in which this historic figure passes through Mequinensa — a detail challenged by the other townspeople.[66]

Certain events in the life of the community of Mequinensa take the form of legends because of the changes and/or amplifications the imagination makes to genuine facts. A good example of this occurs in the writer's first book, to do with a legend about the way the townspeople treat football referees:

> La insòlita ubicació del camp donà lloc també a una llegenda tenaç, apegalosa i escampadissa, segons la qual a la vila llençàvem al riu els àrbitres si la seva actuació no ens agradava. El cronista no negarà que potser, en alguna ocasió, un incontrolat o un grup d'incontrolats o, fins i tot, el públic en pes amenacés l'àrbitre amb un bany intempestiu; també pot concedir que, de vegades, es fessin, en presència del col·legiat, comentaris casuals sobre les dificultats que hi havia per a recuperar els cossos dels malaguanyats que tenien la desgràcia de caure a l'aiguabarreig del Segre i l'Ebre. La veritat, però, és que mai de la vida cap àrbitre no havia anat a parar a l'aigua i la cosa no passava d'un hàbil ardit de la guerra psicològica.[67]
>
> (The unusual location of the pitch also gave rise to a tenacious, persistent and mobile legend, according to which we threw referees into the river if we didn't like their performance. This chronicler would not deny that perhaps, on some occasion, a person or group or even the whole crowd might have got out of control and threatened the referee with a premature bath; I will also admit that, sometimes, they might have made, in the presence of the referee, casual comments about how difficult it was to fish out the bodies of the poor souls who had the misfortune to fall into the confluence of the Segre and Ebro rivers. The truth, though, is that no referee had ever actually ended up in the water and the whole thing was nothing more than a clever trick of psychological warfare.)

The stories 'Absoltes i sepeli de Nicolau Vilaplana' ('Absolution and Burial of Nicolau Vilaplana')[68] and 'Un enigma i set tricornis'[69] describe other episodes in the life of the town connected with football that occupy the status of legends in its memory. The stories and legends carried in the collective memory are therefore characterised by a strong imaginative component, which sometimes leans towards the fantastic.

Song, which is one of the genres of oral literature, is not found very often in Moncada's stories, with one exception. The story entitled 'La lluna, la pruna' ('The moon, the prune')[12] has as its epigraph the words of a popular song, or more precisely a nursery rhyme, which gives Moncada's story its title. Of all his stories, this one and 'Guardeu-vos de somiar genives esdentegades'[71] are the only ones that have a title with a direct link to the popular voice: a song and a superstition, respectively. The title 'La lluna, la pruna' is an ironic nod to the innocence of the character Aristides, the knife-grinder ('l'esmolet') who, after hearing about Neil Armstrong's moon landing, dreams of going to perform the same task on the moon, a new world that, for him, suggests new work opportunities: 'Això de no tenir feina no podia durar gaire. Un món per estrenar, nou de trinca! La d'eines que deu haver-hi per esmolar!' ('He couldn't be out of work for ever. A whole new world to explore, brand new! What a lot of tools must need sharpening there!').[72] The integration of orality in literary discourse, on one hand, and the presence of various oral genres that are either inspired by the collective memory of the real Mequinensa or purely fictional, on the other, lead us to see the work of Jesús Moncada as a 'une ré-écriture savante de la voix' ('an erudite re-writing of the voice'), to use Paul Zumthor's expression.[73]

The Catalan author, with his nostalgia for the living word, has managed — by valuing orality, the privileged vehicle of expression of the collective memory — to contribute to the memory of the language, which is fundamental to a feeling of community belonging. In doing this he has also helped safeguard the linguistic identity of the community of Mequinensa, as was highlighted by the Mayor of the town in one of her speeches following the writer's death: 'La obra de Jesús Moncada hará que nunca más nuestra lengua materna no se lea y escriba en Mequinenza [...]. Las nuevas generaciones tienen un referente sobre nuestra manera de hablar y de vivir' ('The work of Jesús Moncada will mean that it will never again be the case that our maternal language is not read and written in Mequinensa [...]. The new generations have a point of reference for our way of speaking and living.')[74]

Notes

[1] These are: «Conte del vell tramviaire», «L'estremidora confessió de Joe Galaxia» and «Història de dies senars». Jesús Moncada has justified the presence of these texts, which are set in the city, in the volume by the fact that they were written at the same time as the others. (See Mercè Biosca, 'Aproximació a l'obra de Jesús Moncada', *Serra d'Or*, 351 (1989), pp. 55-57.)

[2] This collection also has a general structure that gives it similarities with a novel, since not only is there a prologue whose narrator is one of the characters, but it also ends with an epilogue.

[3] Isidor Cònsul, 'Geografies mítiques', *Lletra de canvi* 31-32 (1990), pp. 11-12.

[4] See Hèctor Moret, 'Aproximació a la toponímia urbana de Mequinensa', in *Actes del Congrès d'Onomàstica (XVII Col·loqui general de la Societat d'Onomàstica — Barcelona : 27, 28, 29 de febrer 1992)*, 1994, pp. 373-381.

[5] Hèctor Moret, '*Camí de sirga*: la recreació d'un món amb nom propi', *La Comarca* (Alcanyís), 26 October 1989, p. 19.

[6] Ada Castells, '20 anys de contes de Jesús Moncada', *Avui* [on line], 12 November 2001, (accessed 08/11/2002).

[7] Philippe Hamon, *L'Ironie littéraire* (Paris: Hachette, 1996), p. 5.

[8] Beda Alleman, 'De l'ironie en tant que principe littéraire', *Poétique (Revue de théorie et d'analyse littéraires)* 36 (1978), p. 389.

[9] 'Cabòries estivals', *El País*, 13 October 1985, Quadern de Cultura, pp. 1-2.

[10] Ramón Acín, 'Jesús Moncada. La alquimia de los recuerdos', *Heraldo de Aragón*, 28 September 1989, Artes y Letras, p.1.

[11] Josep Gras, 'Jesús Moncada: "Sempre he estat un narrador nat"', *Regió 7*, 1 October 1997, Cultures, p. 36.
[12] Alleman, p. 398.
[13] Gras, p. 36.
[14] Lluís Bonada, 'L'humor amera el meu darrer llibre', *El Temps*, 804 (1999), p. 64.
[15] V. Jankelevitch, *L'Ironie* (Paris: Flammarion, 1964) (1st ed. 1936), pp. 130-131, cited in Hamon, p. 109.
[16] V. Július, 'Al nostre gust', *El Temps*, 81 (1986), p. 34. The quotation has been translated by Judith Willis. (See also Estanislau Vidal-Folch, 'Ocupeu una cadira al Cafè de la Granota', *El País*, 26 May 1985, Quadern de Cultura, p. 4.)
[17] Mercè Biosca has produced a synthesis of the use of humour and irony in the author's first three books. (In Emili Bayo and Mercè Biosca, *Guia de lectura de Jesús Moncada* (Barcelona: Edicions de La Magrana, 1992), pp. 71-84).
[18] CDG (Barcelona: La Magrana, 1992), pp. 76-83.
[19] CDG, pp. 50-59.
[20] CDG, pp. 37-42.
[21] Mercè Biosca, 'Noms de casa, renoms i zoònims en l'obra de Jesús Moncada', in *Actes del XIVè Col·loqui General de la Societat d'Onomàstica* (Alacant: Publicacions de la Universitat d'Alacant, 1991), p. 276.
[22] HME (Barcelona: La Magrana, 1993), pp. 128-138.
[23] Hèctor Moret, 'Onomàstica mequinensana en l'obra de Jesús Moncada', *Ilerda "Humanitats"*, LII (1998), pp. 199-214.
[24] Bayo & Biosca, p. 11.
[25] See CDG, p. 40.
[26] See *CdS* (Barcelona: La Magrana, 1994), p. 68. The inhabitants of Mequinensa call this war against Napoleon's troups 'la Guerra del Francés'.
[27] See *CdS*, p. 10.
[28] CA (Barcelona: La Magrana, 1999), pp. 27-34 & 101.
[29] Bayo & Biosca, p. 43.
[30] Hèctor Moret, 'Literatura catalana en Aragón: Jesús Moncada y Desideri Lombarte', in *Actas del II Encuentro "Villa de Benasque" sobre Lenguas y Culturas Pirenaïcas. Benasque (Huesca). 1-4 de septiembre de 1998* (Zaragoza: DGA. Departamento de Educación, Cultura y Deporte, 2003), p. 128.
[31] Mercè Biosca and María Pau Cornadó, 'Jesús Moncada: el riu de la memòria', *Escriptors d'avui* (Lleida: Ajuntament, 1992), p. 50.
[32] HME, pp. 29-38.

[33] In this last part of the prologue it is the narrator-character Mallol Fontcalda who cites these words that the judge Crònides had said to him by way of advice the day after he arrived in Meqinensa.

[34] CA, p. 23.

[35] Isidor Cònsul, 'No badi, cregui'm, això dura poc (La mort en els contes de Jesús Moncada)', *Serra d'Or* 550 (2005), p. 45.

[36] See Rosa María Piñol, 'Entrevista a Jesús Moncada que publica el volumen de relatos *Calaveres atònites*', *La Vanguardia* [online], 22/10/1999.

[37] In a private interview, 18/12/2005.

[38] CA, pp. 5 & 106.

[39] Jesús Moncada, 'Petita història d'un jersei gris', *El Boscater Negre*, November 1988, p. 37.

[40] Biosca and Cornadó, p. 48.

[41] HME, p. 104

[42] HME, p. 107.

[43] See especially Paul Zumthor, 'Entre l'écrit et l'oral', *Les cahiers de Fontenay*, 23 (1981), p. 29.

[44] The term refers to the communion wafer/host and has no translation in English that captures both its literal meaning and use as a swear word.

[45] HME, p. 67.

[46] See the list of examples of coarse or vulgar vocabulary given in Josep Murgades, 'Narrativització de formes simples: l'obra de Jesús Moncada', in *Professor Joaquim Molas: Memòria, Escriptura, Història (vol. II)* (Barcelona: Publicacions de la Universitat de Barcelona, 2003), p. 776.

[47] CDG, p. 51.

[48] CDG, p. 33.

[49] HME, p. 77

[50] CA, p. 226.

[51] Lluís Bonada, 'L'humor amera el meu darrer llibre', *El Temps*, 804 (1999), p. 65.

[52] Mercè Biosca, 'Aproximació a la llengua i a l'estil de Jesús Moncada', in Bayo & Biosca, pp.47-98.

[53] Divergence from the morphosyntactic norm is less common because the author has chosen as a general rule to respect the normative morphosyntaxis of Catalan, such as written form and spelling.

[54] See Mercè Biosca's studies of Moncada's language: Mercè Biosca, *La fraseologia en l'obra de Jesús Moncada*, Estudi General de Lleida (Universitat de Barcelona), 1989 (unpublished), and Biosca,

'Aproximació', pp. 57-63.
[55] Biosca, *La fraseologia,* pp. 57-63.
[56] Ignasi Riera, 'Jesús Moncada, l'art d'un escriptor de café', *Diari de Barcelona*, 14 February 1989, Llibres, p. 8.
[57] HME, p. 59.
[58] CDG, p. 46-47.
[59] CDG, pp. 84-94.
[60] CDG, p. 90.
[61] HME, pp. 60-61
[62] CA, p. 96.
[63] Carles Singla, 'Jesús Moncada recrea la postguerra amb mots amables', *Diari de Barcelona*, 30 January 1992, p. 33.
[64] Xavier Bosch, 'Jesús Moncada escriptor', *Avui*, 26 October 1999, p. 70.
[65] HME, p. 49-50.
[66] CA, pp. 44-45.
[67] CDG, p. 32.
[68] CDG, pp. 17-21.
[69] CDG, pp. 50-59.
[70] HME, pp. 69-78.
[71] CDG, pp. 84-94.
[72] HME, p. 78.
[73] Zumthor, p. 25.
[74] 'Emotiva despedida a Jesús Moncada en Mequinensa', *Heraldo* [on line], 15 June 2005, http://www.heraldo.es/heraldo.html?noticia= 134644, (accessed 16/06/2005).

Old Sheet Music[1]

Translated by Judith Willis

Jordi Ventura, old Uncle Jordi, was a steady, solid sort, a miner with no time for superstitious beliefs involving witches, open scissors, spilled salt, lucky sevens or the devil's tail. But things were to change that evening as he made his way back to the village. In his mind's eye he was already ensconced in his local, Bartomeu's Cafe, with his cronies — Manolet the baker, Atanasi and Dalmau, known as Baskethead — knocking back his Saturday-night rum and singing 'My Sweet Caroline', when a shiver ran down his spine.

The voice came first from behind the old mill by the stagnant ponds, covered in a layer of rotten leaves and dead lizards. It was soft, like an echo in an empty house, and called to him, 'Jordi, Jordi...!'

He brought his cart to a halt and looked around but could see no one. He listened for a few seconds — nothing but the intermittent croaking of the frogs down by the river. He chose to ignore it and with a flick of the rope started his mule off again.

The windows of the village were already visible above the olive groves in the wine-coloured evening light when the voice rang out again, 'Jordi, Jordi...!'

This time he started to feel alarmed. There was something familiar about the voice, as if known to him from many years ago. He tried hard to remember and as it found a name and a body in the world of memories, Jordi Ventura shuddered. It was the voice of his uncle, Uncle Anselm, who used to take him to his smallholding when he was a little boy and who had been dead for over forty years.

And then, after his uncle, he heard his grandfather calling him, 'Jordi, Jordi...!'

At this point he had to hold on tight to the edge of his cart to stop himself falling under the wheels. He shut his eyes. The voices grew fainter and floated upwards, towards the family graves where the withered flowers from last All Saints' Day stood next to the oil lamps, the votive candles and the faded photos.

Uncle Jordi feared he would never make it to the village. In the few yards remaining, his horse would age and waste away, its skin stretched tight and its ribs jutting out. It would stumble forward with its mouth open until it dropped dead, its yellow teeth fixed in a bitter grimace. And he, Jordi, would be stuck like a scarecrow on his cart with no hope of jumping off, shouting or moving — he would never move again. He would feel long ashen whiskers sprout on his sunken cheeks and the wind slowly cover him in earth. The soil would gradually fill in the deep furrows of his wrinkles, bury his old sandals, get inside the pocket of his dark shirt and finally bring his watch to a standstill. And one day, in many years' time, when the rainwater had rotted his cart and he lay flat on the ground, the autumn wind would blow corn seeds into his ears.

The cart creaked to a halt.

'The mule will fall now', thought Jordi. 'It's all over.'

Suddenly he heard the sound of voices. He opened his eyes in dread and found himself in front of Bartomeu's Cafe. Inside his friends were singing 'My Sweet Caroline'.

'My sweet Caroline
Has left me for a sailor boy.'

Bartomeu's Cafe. Old tables, wobbly chairs and that Saturday-night smell of coffee, alcohol and black tobacco. There they all were, drinking, singing, playing cards. All enjoying themselves. The only discordant note came from the parrot, a scraggy green bird with a rasping, heavy drinker's voice, perched beside what was left of an old calendar for a brand of anisette from before the war. It screeched in despair, 'Paca! Where are you Paca my love? Paca, oh Paca!' The bird could feel the ringworm eating away at its feathers, leaving the shafts exposed, and could see the cobwebs slowly and patiently weaving a bridge between the bottles on the shelves and the yellow light bulb, and enveloping Bartomeu, frozen in another time. Only the parrot noticed the plaster flaking silently off the walls and smelled the black haze that floated in the old cafe and presaged collapse and ruin. Its instinct told it which beam would crash down and flatten it and which playing card would be found creased in its master's hand the day they were both carried out of the debris of that world of memories. And that's why it screeched 'Paca, oh Paca...!' amidst strangled squawks and noises like a coffee grinder to the one-time girlfriend of the landlord, knowing full well she would never be back.

'The days are so long
So long since she's been gone,
That sweetheart of mine.
Tell me, where did you go
And where are you now,
My sweet Caroline?'

'All right, Atanasi, that's enough of your booming. We've had more than our fair share of thunder this year!'

'Be quiet, you numbskull!'

Uncle Jordi, leaning on the bar alongside his friends, was plunged in deep sorrow. But he tried hard to give nothing away. He talked and smoked, seeking in vain to forget what had happened. Since the events on his way there, nothing was the same. It felt as if a curtain had fallen between him and the world — as everyday colours, voices and movements passed through, their significance was filtered out and he was left with nothing but cold, muted colours, empty voices and jerky, meaningless movements. He felt the same sense of isolation as when he was a boy and stood in the empty village square beneath the tattered streamers on the last night of the town festival, watching the musicians pack up their instruments and go off to another festival which would also come to an end under the gaze of another adolescent boy.

'Jordi', the voice of Joan the builder came to him from far off, sounding empty. 'How many of the constable's teeth did you knock out that night you had a scrap?'

'No idea.'

'When I swept the floor the next morning I found four', volunteered Bartomeu.

'But how many more did he swallow?' asked Joan, goading him on.

'He spent two months eating nothing but hot soup!'

There was a silence but Jordi realized in horror that they were all still talking. Their hands and lips were moving, but he no longer formed part of their world. Dalmau, 'Baskethead', opened his black, toothless mouth in what must have been a laugh that he couldn't hear. Because all he could hear was the voice, the voice from earlier, calling to him through the cafe door. 'Jordi, Jordi...!'

He held onto the bar, trembling. And at that moment he heard Dalmau laugh.

'What can I get you?' asked Manolet the baker. 'It's on me so make the most of it!'

'A glass of brandy.'

'A tot of rum for me!'

'Black coffee with a dash of bleach!'

'I'm in no mood for riddles tonight. So coffee all round', ruled Bartomeu, annoyed because he'd been playing patience all evening without winning.

'That's democracy for you!'

The voice couldn't be after him. He wasn't an old man yet, he was still strong, still at work. Look at his hands — they had never once rested. He raised them as if to show them to an invisible person and was petrified. What sinister game was this? Who had changed his big, strong hands into these young boy's hands? But once he got over his initial shock, he realized that they were not unfamiliar to him and recalled the sweet feeling in those tender little fingers which were just starting to recognize things: the chair, the table, the key to his parents' house, the copper candlestick, the mysterious sewing table in the kitchen, crammed with fascinating buttons, cotton reels, long needles and faded pictures from memorial cards; the spectacles belonging to his grandad, that big strong man with a crook, a silver watch and a dog called Quinto. His fingers brought back all these things he once knew — the iron pick his father used to tear coal from the mine was cold, his mother's face was soft and gentle, and you mustn't play with the logs on the fire or with knives because if you did, the fairies wouldn't leave chocolate under your pillow.

Atanasi's loud voice broke the spell. 'What did you put in the coffee today, Bartomeu you old devil?'

'Don't tell me, I can guess', shouted another voice. 'The priest's socks!'

'In mine there was a chicken in spectacles!'

'And in mine, a roly-poly toy with pockets!'

'Aren't you all lucky? I just got the vicar's Sunday-school cane.'

'If you don't watch out, I'll lose my temper and then you'll be sorry! What's the matter with my coffee?'

Full of nostalgia, Uncle Jordi looked at his hands: the fairies and those lovely long summers were now long gone. His still soft hands were gripped round the handle of a spade, grimy with coal dust; his mother's home-made soap made his chapped hands sore. They grew broader and harder by the day. They learned how to roll cigarettes without tearing the paper or dropping the tobacco, how to shake hands properly, on Saturday evenings how to shave his face clean with his father's razor and how to rap on the table during the card games at Bartomeu's Cafe. They got nervous when they clasped the waist of a pretty girl at the local hop or when mysterious ladies with heavily made-up eyes swooned in the arms of Rudolph Valentino on the sheet that passed for a screen in the village fleapit. All the hands he knew were friendly hands — those of the sailors who rowed down the Ebro to the sea in barges laden with coal, the miners whose hands were like his, the caulkers, peasants and builders. And best of all, those of Manolet the baker who would sit on the sacks of flour in the rosemary-scented air playing his trombone and reading Bakunin while the bread baked in the oven. Jordi could still see his hands breaking into applause at the cafe run by a young Bartomeu thirty years ago as the lights went down amidst shouts and cheers and then Paca la Xina burst onto the brightly-lit stage in a low-cut outfit topped off by a blue striped scarf on her head. She started to sing, accompanied on the maracas by a black man in a straw hat and floral braces, straight out of an advertisement for chocolate. Now he could see clearly that Manolet was the only one to realize in all that excitement that the cabaret singer was the dying breath of an age that was coming to an end, and that very soon the stage would fall dark forever.

'Where are you Paca? Paca, oh Paca...!

'Bloody parrot...'

The others had all finished their coffee. His was the only cup left on the bar and it had gone cold. But Uncle Jordi didn't notice. His eyes saw nothing but his 22-year old hands, idle and full of rage. The mines had been shut down. The barges no longer sailed down the river to the sea but like black, putrid fish they rotted in the silence of the river or on the banks; the scorching white sun cracked them open with a sinister groan and grey willows grew among their timbers. Gone was the noise of the caulkers' adzes and the voices of the shipowners. The silence became tangible, unbearable in the burning hot streets where the only living soul was a collarless dog, most likely a stray. And then his hands grasped the rifle. They still recalled its weight and shape, the cold contact of the bolt. In the trenches, the hands of his comrades: rough and smooth, strong and trembling, much missed. Those of 'Baskethead' Dalmau, thrust deep inside the pockets of his militiaman's boiler suit, those of Manolet the baker writing letters for Bartomeu to send to Paca la Xina, who had been left on her own, her eye make-up smudged and running with the tears of farewells, in the cafe now emptied of people, noise and music and where cobwebs hung from the beams. He saw his hands on that hellish day of the counterattack at Singra and remembered Manolet's calm voice in the thick of battle, 'How's it going, Jordi?'

'How's it going, Jordi?'

Jordi jumped. For a second he'd thought he was still there and could see the battalion commander's red stripe on Manolet's shirt. But it wasn't that. Time had passed and he'd heard a voice calling him.

'Fine, Manolet, just fine.'

'Aren't you going to drink your coffee? It must be cold by now...'

He couldn't. He tried again in despair while glancing sideways at his friends who were talking about women.

'I took hold of her...', bragged Dalmau.

'Behind the door?', said Atanasi, spurring him on.

'How did you guess?'

'Because you've been doing it in the same place for fifty years.'

'What do you mean?

'Just that there's a proper way to do things.'

Jordi couldn't understand what was happening. He gritted his teeth and tried once more to pull his hands apart and pick up his cup of coffee from the bar. He felt a terrible burning pain in his wrists and nearly cried out loud. At that same moment he saw the rope, the rope they'd used when they took him prisoner. Now, thirty years on, it was still tied fast. He pulled on it furiously, snapping it, and as he did so his right fist dashed his coffee cup onto the floor, where it shattered on the tiles.

'Don't worry, Jordi, it will all come right in time', someone said.

That was easy to say but what did it mean? That night time meant nothing — it was like the old calendar with the dates all torn off hanging next to the raucous parrot. There was no distance, no separation between the hands which had just broken the cup and those feverish, emaciated hands which rediscovered all the familiar objects in March 1940 on his release from the concentration camp. What joy, mingled with sadness and fear, ran through his fingers as they brushed against the door of his home, the grief-stricken, anxious face of his mother, the face of his father, grown old and serious, the crook of his grandfather who had died while he was far away! And in the cafe, the same cafe where he found himself today, how strange to feel the hands of his friends. Some broken, empty, flabby, defeated; others whole and strong. And the hands of the invisible absentees which came from afar, from the graveyards of Teruel, Singra, Upper Aragon, like a breath, just next to his... There was 'Baskethead' Dalmau, Atanasi, Manolet the baker kneading black bread now and no longer playing his trombone because the famished rats in the bakery had eaten up his sheet music while he was away.

The cafe was sad, lifeless. On the counter, silhouetted against a background of empty dusty shelves, sat chattering a green parrot which Bartomeu had brought back from France for Paca la Xina. But she had left the village. She'd gone along with everyone else the day it was evacuated and no one had heard from her since. And the parrot called her, mimicking in its rum-soaked voice the laments of the cafe owner, 'Paca, Where are you Paca my darling? Paca, oh Paca!'

'Paca, Where are you Paca my darling? Paca, oh Paca!'

Jordi had to force himself not to jump over the bar and throttle the bird to silence forever that hopeless cry that bored into his brain. But he stopped himself. He understood that if he killed the parrot he would also kill Bartomeu and scatter the dust of those memories which made him live.

'Are we going to see any rum this evening?', exclaimed Dalmau. 'How many are there of us? Two, four, six, not counting Atanasi because he's a reactionary, nine. Thirteen in all.'

'Unlucky for some!'

'Don't worry. My father always said a man shouldn't be scared until he sees his own head four steps in front of him. Bartomeu, rum for twenty-four!'

Uncle Jordi didn't even touch his glass. As he reached for it he heard the voice calling him again from the square, 'Jordi, Jordi...' And the echo inside his head said 'Old, old!' Old?

It was only yesterday that his loving hands caressed the quivering body of Maria, only yesterday that they stroked little Dora's fair plaits tied with sky-blue ribbons. He thought, however, with a shudder, that his daughter had been a woman for a long time now. He remembered when Maria told him — those days when his daughter was pale and looked embarrassed and would cry for no reason. He remembered too the mixture of pride and fear that filled his heart and saw his hands awkwardly veer away from his daughter's plaits, not knowing quite what to do and fiddle instead with his father's watch chain, which had graced his own waistcoat for the past fourteen years.

The deep anguish he felt began to weigh heavy in his heart. Jordi needed to stop that voice, cut it off and be himself again, the man who only that afternoon had been sitting on the cart, daydreaming about his friends and his glass of rum, with the tender joy of being alive, a man with hope. He understood, though, that he wouldn't do this by staying inside, in the old cafe of the past, bemoaning with Bartomeu the disappearance of the artiste, who would never sing again.

He must leave, climb aboard the cart which was waiting outside and carry on.

'My sweet Caroline
Has left me for a sailor boy.'

They were all drunk. The baker, who never drank and stood like a sentinel on duty, was the only one to see him leave.

The creak of the cafe door as it closed behind him echoed like a long groan through the deep gloom that pervaded the arcade around the square. As he left, Jordi had an idea of what lay ahead and when the silence in the square confirmed his utter solitude, he felt weak, helpless, cowardly. He wanted to go back inside the cafe. But he was too ashamed.

He walked over to the cart. But suddenly as he was about to climb in, it split in two, as if he were seeing double, and he was faced with two carts. They were identical — the same wheels, the same colour, the same old horse tied to the shafts. He was overcome with anxiety; he knew he had no choice but to get into one of them. He couldn't stay in the square or go back inside Bartomeu's cafe. He guessed that one of the carts would take him to a village of smoke and mists inhabited by people with no name and no shadow, where the clocks had no hands, and the other would take him back to hope, to life, to himself. But he also knew it was pointless to try and guess which was which. No one had ever found the answer to the question that was burning within him.

In the cafe the rough, rum-soaked voices were gradually falling silent. Only 'Baskethead', who had collapsed behind the bar at the feet of the pensive baker, had the strength to reach the last verse:

'The days are so long
So long since she's been gone,

That sweetheart of mine.'

And as the cart could be heard rolling away outside, the parrot put an end to the chorus,

'Tell me, where did you go,
My sweet Caroline?'

Notes

[1] Jesús Moncada, 'D'uns vells papers de musica', *Històries de la mà esquerra*, first published 1981.

Chapter 4

The Novels: Myth, History, Storytelling and Memory
Kathryn Crameri

Jesús Moncada published just three novels: *Camí de sirga* (1988), *La galeria de les estàtues* (1992), and *Estremida memòria* (1997). A fourth novel, provisionally titled *Dante, Societat Anònima* (Dante, Limited) remained unfinished at the time of his death in 2005 and is unlikely to be published posthumously.[1] Moncada did not publish prolifically because he liked to revise his work thoroughly before declaring it ready for public consumption. Nevertheless, the three novels had a major impact on Catalan literature and earned Moncada a reputation as one of the greatest contemporary novelists working in Catalan. Just as importantly, *Camí de sirga* was translated into many European and Asian languages and has come to be appreciated by readers from a wide range of countries — a remarkable achievement for a text that has such firm cultural roots.

It is very tempting to treat all three novels as part of one coherent saga, or at least as narrating tales from the same fictional universe. This is mainly because of the definite placing of the novels in a specific setting — Aragón — and a specific time, roughly a century and a half of Spain's modern history up to the end of the twentieth century. In all three novels, narration of events in the present is complemented with flashbacks to the past, either to a specific time (1877 in the case of *Estremida memòria,* and the Civil War in *La galeria de les estàtues*) or to a range of historical periods, as in the case in *Camí de sirga*. This also means that memory is one of the key themes of the novels, as they examine how both communities and individuals store and recall the events that define their past and present. Information about the past is always filtered and distorted, firstly because of attempts to cover over painful episodes at the time they occur, and secondly because of the weaknesses of human memory itself.

Another important element in making the three novels seem like part of a coherent whole is Moncada's technique of characterisation. Just like his short stories, the novels are populated with a large number of major and minor characters who are very skilfully drawn and have a wide variety of functions. Sometimes, for example, a character is introduced briefly in order to perform a comic function, such as Atanasi Costa in *Camí de sirga* who is seen carrying his own coffin back to the coffin-maker in order to ask for a refund after he had erroneously been certified dead by the local doctor. In this case, Atanasi's presence also has a more serious impact since we are told at the end of this comic episode that he died 'for real' in exile in France after the Civil War. In other cases, characters also shift the point of view of the narration, giving a different perspective on events and challenging the reader not to take everything at face value. This is the explicit role of Arnau de Roda in *Estremida memòria* as he comments on the account of the events of 1877 being written by the author Jesús. However, many characters perform this function in less obvious ways, either in dialogue or through the narration of their thoughts, or because they take on the role of narrator for a short while so that we see things from a different perspective.

One of the reasons for the distinctiveness of Moncada's characters is the language in which they are described. His reputation as a novelist has been built partly on his dexterity with the Catalan language, and this can be seen in all areas of his work: names of characters and places, dialogue, descriptions, narration, humour and irony. Moncada was born in

Mequinensa and therefore grew up speaking what is known as 'North-Western' Catalan, as opposed to the 'Central' version that is regarded as the standard dialect. Some of the vocabulary and phrases he uses are particular to Western Catalan, but as Ramon Sistac has pointed out, it is an error to think of Moncada as writing entirely in that dialect since he only uses certain features of it at opportune moments.[2] Nevertheless his prose is incredibly rich and uses a very wide vocabulary. One of the most obvious features of his command of language is his way with names and nicknames, many of which are colourful, ironic, or symbolic. The novels are peppered with characters with such names as Arquimedes Quintana, Melquíades, Genís Borbó, or nicknames like Sil·logisme Mortal, Nelson, and Sèmola.

All of these aspects will be explored in this chapter, firstly by looking at each of the novels in turn, and then by drawing together the themes and techniques that connect them.

Camí de sirga (1988)

Moncada's first novel has become his best known and is the one for which he will be most remembered. Having already published two collections of short stories, Moncada built on these to produce a fuller fictionalisation of the real town of Mequinensa around which they had been based. The pivotal event in the novel is the destruction of the town in 1970-1 in order to construct a dam that would provide hydro-electric power. The project had been in the pipeline since 1957, which meant that the townspeople had been living for some time with the knowledge that they would have to leave their homes. The destruction of the town, when it finally begins, provides the stimulus for telling the stories of Mequinensa's past — stories which, it is implied, may well be lost with the town.[3] This means that there is only a very simple, and almost incidental, overarching plot, provided by real historical events. The interest is in the sub-plots: the tales that are woven around this simple framework.

These tales concern a large number of characters and relate different incidents in Mequinensa's modern history, concentrating on the period from the First World War to the point at which the town was destroyed. While there are no principal protagonists in the sense of people that we follow constantly throughout the book, there are many that are present at different points: the sailors Arquimedes Quintana and 'Nelson', the upper-middle class Carlota de Torres, the ill-fated Aleix de Segarra, etc. Many of the characters can be grouped either by family associations (e.g. the Torres, Camps or Salleres families), workplaces (the river, the mines, or employees of different households), or the places in which they spend their leisure time (the Eden cabaret, the Cafè del Moll, or the Casino de la Roda). These associations also tell us something about a particular character's social status and likely political stance, since there is a clear division in the town between the owners of the businesses and their employees. The owners belong to wealthy families who glory in their high status and are more likely to hold conservative views, whereas the workers are more likely to hold left-wing views. As Emili Bayo points out, Carlota de Torres is the main representative of the first group, and Nelson of the second, since they appear throughout the novel and are present for most of the chronological span of the narration, especially its closing chapters.[4]

The large number of characters that appear in the novel encourages us to think of the stories we are reading as representing a collective, so that the town of Mequinensa takes on a greater significance than simply being the backdrop for a series of individual lives. This is one of the reasons why critics have spoken of Moncada as creating a 'myth of Mequinensa' and have compared it to García Márquez's famous Macondo of *Cien años de soledad* (a comparison Moncada himself thought was incorrect, especially when it was extended to include elements of magic realism).[5] Another reason for this sense of significance is the mythical resonances of the structure of the novel, since the destruction of the town by flooding after its gradual decline over many decades inevitably leads to comparisons with 'fall and flood' myths such as those of Noah's Ark or Atlantis.[6] Another myth is deliberately highlighted by Moncada by his choice of 'Eden' as the name of the cabaret that operated in Mequinensa during the prosperous years of the First World War. The decline that followed the end of the war marked the end of prosperity and therefore the end of this particular 'Garden of Eden', but the last section of the novel in which the inhabitants leave the town forever could also be said to have echoes of an expulsion from Eden.[7]

Moncada's use of myth will be explored in greater detail later in this chapter, but it is worth noting here that one of the main ways in which the myth of Mequinensa is created is through the storytelling activities of its inhabitants. In many ways, the townspeople actually create a myth of — and for — themselves. They do this by creating versions of events that hide some of their more unsavoury aspects and instead present them in ways that show the townspeople in a good light.[8] These versions then pass into the collective memory, becoming part of the identity of the town. The way in which communities construct their own autobiography through selective remembering and forgetting is a major theme of both *Camí de sirga* and *Estremida memòria*.

It is interesting that despite the importance of myth, historical events are also vital to frame and underpin the events occurring in Mequinensa itself. In many cases these involve wars, from the Battle of Tetuan in 1860, through to the First World War, the Spanish Civil War, and the Second World War. All of these have real and direct consequences for the town and its people. Arquimedes Quintana lost an ear at Tetuan, the First World War brings prosperity to Mequinensa as the mines go into overdrive, and the Civil War represents a collective defeat for the town which had been staunchly Republican. The Second World War, although a distant event compared with the

Spanish disaster that immediately proceeded it, still has a direct impact on Mequinensa by claiming the lives of some of its former residents. These historical events serve to anchor the fictional stories of the people of Mequinensa in time and space, and help the reader to make sense of the different levels of time that the novel narrates. From the events of 1970-1, we are transported — as the destruction of each house jogs the memories of the surviving Mequinensans — through the modern history of the town until we arrive at the final moment in its existence. Although Moncada himself stressed that he was not writing a history of the town 'si més no en el sentit usual del mot' ('at least not in the usual sense of the word'),[9] this use of history gives the stories of *Camí de sirga* a greater impact and serves to remind us of the real Mequinensa that was lost under the waters in 1971.

La galeria de les estàtues (1992)

In his second novel, Moncada moves partly away from the setting that had proved so crucial to the success of *Camí de sirga* by creating a fictional town — Torrelloba — that some readers have identified with Zaragoza. Certainly, there are similarities between the setting of the novel and Moncada's own experience of being a trainee teacher in Zaragoza. However, the question of whether Torrelloba 'is' Zaragoza is largely irrelevant. More important is the contrast that is drawn between the haughty and indifferent Torrelloba and the close community of Mequinensa, which provides a second location for events. The 'present' time of the novel is 1957, and this is shown once again by reference to a historical event: the war in Ifni. Indeed most of the action of the novel takes place between the beginning of the civil war and this 'forgotten war'.

The novel is basically a family saga and pivots around one young man, Dalmau Campells, whose father was killed during the Civil War in unknown circumstances. Dalmau, who was brought up in Mequinensa with his mother, sister and other family members, is desperate to find out what happened to his father, and although the reader eventually learns the truth, Dalmau ironically never does. Instead he meets a similar fate to his father: he is killed needlessly by someone he knows and ought to have been able to trust. This means that as well as being a family saga the novel also has elements of a detective story. Dalmau's search for the truth about his father is one element in this, but throughout the novel we are also following a group of policemen as they go about their business and, eventually, investigate the murder of Dalmau. The most important of these characters is Inspector Melquíades, who is drawn into the tragedy himself when he finds out that his daughter has been secretly seeing Dalmau's cousin, Ferran. It is Ferran's desertion from the army for fear of being sent to fight in Africa that leads directly to the tragic deaths of Dalmau, his attacker, the policeman Cabrera, Inspector Melquíades, and the director of the college where Ferran and Dalmau were studying.

One of the main features of the novel is precisely the way that all these disparate characters turn out to be linked through both events and personal relationships. The first part of the novel introduces a large number of characters, but at this stage we are not told that they are all interrelated and form part of the web of events that will eventually lead to tragedy. Suspense is deliberately cultivated by Moncada in different ways, as we piece together information from the narration. For example, there are references to a group of blind people converging on Torrelloba that seem to have no link to the rest of the events, and it is only near the very end of the novel that their role is revealed as 'witnesses' to the killing of Sub-Inspector Cabrera. Another tactic revolves around the use of both nicknames and proper names to describe the characters, in some cases in order to hide the fact that what appears to be two people is actually the same person. The most important case of this is Melquíades daughter 'la Loló' who turns out to be Ferran's girlfriend Esther.[10] We do not find out the connection until Melquíades himself does. Moncada also uses other tactics to keep information from the reader until its significance is clear. One example of this is that we find out late in the novel that the director of Dalmau's college is the brother of the Republican activist Laura who was close friends with Dalmau's father. The sheer quantity of characters and the gradual revelation of links between them makes certain demands on the reader, who may feel confused by so many gobbets of information.

The personal relationships between the characters are complicated by their positions within the Nationalist/Republican divide. Dalmau's family is a good example of the kinds of bitter divisions families suffered during the Civil War, since his uncle Bernat was a Nationalist but his sister — Dalmau's mother — married a Republican. However, some of the divisions are not clear cut, and the characters are complex rather than being defined solely by their political allegiances. Bernat, for example, joins the Nationalists largely by accident, having gone after the initial uprising in Torrelloba to ask a family friend (Commandant Ribera) whether it was possible for him to get back to Mequinensa.[11] We see that Bernat later uses his position to try to help those who were regarded as 'enemies' after the war, ensuring that they are sheltered from some of the worst excesses of the Francoist reprisals.[12] On the other hand, Dalmau's death at the hands of a fellow student who belonged to an extreme right-wing group shows the persistence of these divisions twenty years later, despite the hope of the director of the college (known to his students as Sil·logisme Mortal) that 'els fills dels que van caure lamentablement en l'error redimeixin ara el pecat dels pares' ('the sons and daughters of those who committed an unfortunate error will now redeem the sins of their parents').[13]

This wish points to a naturalistic aspect of this novel, since the tragedy at the end is presented as an inevitable result of the deep divisions in Spanish society. The implication is that when a society is rotten at the core, innocence is no guarantee that your own life will not be touched by evil. Dalmau's death was in fact preventable, if Melquíades and Cabrera had not been held up in traffic and had arrived earlier at the museum in whose statue gallery Dalmau's murder occurs. Yet his death is also presented as inevitable, since it mirrors the cycle that led to the death of his father. Also, the final tragedy is not just confined to the death of Dalmau but spirals out of control to produce four violent deaths and one suicide. This again shows how intimately each individual in a community is linked, with no one able to escape the consequences of such a seismic social rift.

In fact, one of the keys to understanding the novel is precisely to see how the lack of a sense of community in Torrelloba contributes to these individual tragedies. There are two aspects to this problem: the enforced lack of information generated by the machinery of the Franco regime, and the proud and indifferent attitude of the people of Torrelloba who are in fact happy to believe the propaganda. One of the minor characters in the novel is the journalist Gomis whose job is futile as he is not allowed to report on most of the things that he knows have happened.[14] Even the deaths of Dalmau, his attacker and Sub-Inspector Cabrera are not reported.[15] As a result, the people believe that they live in a decent society where crime is minimal, and they have no desire to question this, preferring to think of themselves as inhabitants of 'l'ínclita, catòlica i gairebé immortal ciutat de Torrelloba' ('the illustrious, catholic and almost immortal city of Torrelloba').[16] For those who have read *Camí de sirga* before coming to *La galeria de les estàtues* there is a clear contrast between the portrayal of the strong and interdependent society of Mequinensa in the first novel, and the indifference and individualism of Torrelloba presented in the second. The implication is that Torrelloba is not able to form the kind of community memories that would make it a cohesive society, and that its people would not want to even if they could, preferring the false sense of cohesion that comes with ignorance.

Estremida memòria (1997)

Moncada's third novel returns both to Mequinensa and to the theme of the relationship between memory and collective identity. As with the previous two novels, different layers of time are involved, and in this case this means both a 'present' and a 'past' that have very specific dates: the years 1995 and 1877 respectively. A writer living in late-twentieth century Barcelona, Jesús, has been sent by a close family friend a report written by a court scribe on a trial that took place in Mequinensa in 1877. The trial was a highly significant event in the history of Mequinensa as it involved four of the townspeople being accused of a robbery which involved the murder not just of strangers but of a fellow Mequinensan, Artur. The crime is so shocking and its consequences so divisive that the town constructs a version of the events which minimizes its impact on them and on future generations. When Jesús starts to dig for information, his interventions open old wounds and the townspeople once again attempt to close ranks around the issue.

There is no doubt that the four accused men did commit the crime: Genís Borbó, Valentí Calsina, Feliu Noguera and Simó Juneda first of all deny their involvement but eventually confess, and there is clear evidence of their guilt. More important is the question of whether their trials are fair and whether the punishment they receive — execution — is justified in all cases. The implication is that in order to remove the stain of the crime from the town, the people of Mequinensa collaborate in a miscarriage of justice designed to demonstrate that they have disowned the four men and to bury the matter as quickly as possible. The court scribe, Agustí Montolí, is one of those who becomes persuaded that the trial was unfair and tries to intervene before the executions. However, very few people want to hear his reasons and he is even beaten up for interfering.[17] There is no desire to explore the complexities of the situation because this will prolong the matter and throw up secrets that the townspeople are desperately trying to keep buried.

The narrative structure of the novel is different from that of the two previous ones in that it includes, after every few chapters, letters that comment on what has gone before. The letters are from the family friend who originally gave Jesús the scribe's report, Arnau de Roda, and his daughter Palmira. As Jesús writes, he sends them the manuscript for their comments. This is important to the theme of the novel as it sets up a tension between Jesús's account of events and the perspective that Arnau has on them, thanks to information passed down from his grandfather Ulises. Arnau often adds further points, or suggests that Jesús's version is not quite accurate or should focus on something different. This demonstrates how hard it is to know the truth so many years after everything happened, because even though the scribe's written report seems to have more legitimacy than Arnau's second-hand memories, Arnau is often adamant about certain details.

For example, he advises Jesús to add more detail to a scene in which Emília goes to find out whether her friend's husband, Feliu, had really been at a farm at the other end of the district when the crime took place. In Jesús's account Emília merely leaves the house for a while and then comes back with the news that the owner of the farm has said that Feliu was definitely not there at that time.[18] Arnau wants Jesús to describe Emília's visit to the gentlemen's club to find the owner, and the scandal she caused by walking into the club. Not only that, but he adds details that are meant to heighten the tension of the episode and bring more atmosphere to it.[19] For example, he adds some descriptive touches of colour to the scene, but this is picked up on by Palmira in one of her customary short notes at the end of her father's letter. The observer who saw Emília go to the *Casino*, she says, was colour-blind, and could not therefore have described such detailed hues when relaying the scene to Arnau's grandfather, who must have added them to the account himself.[20] The narrative technique of adding comments through the device of the letters is therefore used to cast doubt on the whole question of the reliability of memory and the truthfulness of any account, even if supplied by a direct witness.

The issue of truth is fundamental to Jesús's quest to find out as much as possible about events, and of course also to the question of whether the four men deserved to die for their crimes. In fact, Genís de Borbó is shot trying to escape when the prisoners are passing the scene of the crime on the way back to Mequinensa from their trial in Casp. There are three versions of this story, two of which are related to the mysterious fact of Genís's royal surname.[21] According to the townspeople, either he was shot in order to avoid the embarrassment of a Bourbon being publicly executed, or because the Guàrdia Civil was worried that he would be pardoned (for the same reason) and took the law into their own hands. These are the more exotic versions of the story that circulate a century later, not the simpler explanation that he simply broke down when they reached the spot on the road where the crime occurred, and tried to flee in terror at what he had done. This particular episode indicates two things: that we tend to prefer to remember the exotic over the prosaic, and that different versions of a story can still coexist as long as they are compatible with the general restrictions imposed by the workings of collective memory.

One of the key themes of the novel, then, is the way the town of Mequinensa constructs a story to minimise the impact of the crime on its self-image. Jesús's intervention is so unwelcome because his investigations shine a light on this process, revealing how and why the majority of the townspeople colluded in it. Also, there were many other personal misdemeanours that individuals fought to keep hidden at the time, worried that the spotlight on Mequinensa generated by the crime would reach into their own private lives. The effect of this 'cover-up operation' is to leave the townspeople's image of themselves as untouched as possible. As we will see later in this chapter, the idea that the Mequinensans are something of a special group compared with other towns in the area is one of the defining features of Moncada's novels and contributes to the mythification of Mequinensa in his work.

Themes: Myth, History, Memory and Storytelling

It will be apparent from this description of the three novels that the themes of myth, history, memory and storytelling are woven into the fabric of Moncada's fictional universe. They are present in the structure of the narration as well as being explored through characters and events. The aim of this part of the chapter is to show how this is achieved. To do this, I will be taking examples from all three novels, bearing in mind my earlier comment that the internal consistency of their settings allows us to treat them in this way.

As has already been pointed out, the most obvious occurrence of myth in Moncada's work is the way that Mequinensa itself — not just the fictional version, but in some ways the real town too — has been elevated to the status of a mythical place. This is the result of several things, including the fact that Mequinensa's gradual destruction and final flooding automatically leads to comparisons with 'fall and flood' myths, and the way Moncada himself highlights comparisons with the Garden of Eden in *Camí de sirga*. However, this is only the backdrop to a more complex exploration of the creation of collective myths through storytelling that we see in all three novels. On a simple level, for instance, this could be seen in the way that the Franco regime operated through creating myths about Spain, which is explored in *La galeria de les estàtues* (the myth of a crime-free society, for example, which is achieved by controlling the stories told by the press). However, it is not just institutions that have their own myth-making tendencies but individuals and groups too. They are able to control the way they portray themselves to others by telling their own stories in certain ways. In doing this they create versions of their life-stories that are as much myth as history.

The exploration of this process is one of the most important features of Moncada's work. Mequinensa as he portrays it is differentiated from other towns around it by its strong cohesion as a group, something which Moncada has said was a feature of the real town before it was destroyed. In an interview published in 1999 he commented that the people of Mequinensa 'tenia un tarannà social que contrastava molt amb tota la resta' and explains this by the fact that 'Mequinensa era un poble unànimement republicà i d'esquerres' ('a social make-up that contrasted greatly with all the rest', 'Mequinensa was unanimously Republican and left-wing.')[22] In his fiction, Moncada explores some of the mechanisms by which this sense of unity is created.

As an example of this we can look at one of the specific incidents in *Camí de sirga*. During the Carlist wars, an old cannon is pressed into service to defend the town, and one night it is fired at what is thought to be a group of attackers, who are apparently heroically defeated. The next morning, however, there is no trace of them. Realising that there had been no attack, the townspeople are in danger of looking ridiculous, until the local surgeon suggests that maybe the bodies of the enemy had all been swallowed up by the river. 'En sentir les paraules del cirurgià, a més d'un heroi van acudir-li a l'esment els crits d'agonia o la xiuladissa sinistra de les bales que venien de la fosca, desapercebuts la nit abans.' ('On hearing the surgeons' words, several of the heroes recollected the screams of agony or the sinister noise of the bullets whizzing out of the darkness, which had gone unnoticed the night before.').[23] This idea solves the problem and is enthusiastically adopted as the version that will pass into history.

In some ways, the actions of the townspeople in *Estremida memòria* represent a more protracted and intricate version of the same tactic. The crime of the four Mequinensans risks spoiling the reputation of the town by making all of its inhabitants — the neighbours, friends, family and lovers of the men — guilty by association. If the strength of this association can be reduced by showing that the men were 'not really' part of the town, then the damage to the collective identity can be kept to a minimum. In the words of Garrigues the ferryman, 'Mequinensa no en té la culpa, que no se li pot carregar el que va ser obra de quatre bojos' ('Mequinensa isn't at fault, you can't blame it for the actions of four madmen').[24] It is this process of disowning the men that allows the miscarriage of justice to happen, but the unspoken view is that this is for the greater good of the town.

While these examples of myth-making rely on deliberate or semi-deliberate manipulations of the collective life-history, there is another factor that Moncada explores that is a more subtle contributor to the workings of myth: the fallibility of human memory. Research by psychologists into the way autobiographical memory works has shown that it has the ability to trick us into believing that what we remember is totally accurate, but in fact it is very unlikely to be correct except in its broad outline. This is partly because memories of a single event are often composites of many similar events, put together as a 'flavour' of what one instance could have plausibly been like. Moncada gives a very clear example of this in *Camí de sirga* when Carlota de Torres remembers a band playing in the town on the occasion of the declaration of the Second Republic in 1931.[25] Forty years on, the one detail she remembers most clearly is actually false: the trombone she can hear standing out from the rest of the band was not really there. In fact, we are told by the narrator, there had not been a trombone in the band since the time of the First World War. By placing the trombone in the band of 1931, Carlota is unconsciously evoking more pleasant memories of prosperous times rather than the uncertain era of the 1930s.

Another characteristic of human memory is that, by retelling the story of things that have happened to us we tend to introduce changes that become part of the memory we hold of the event itself. *Camí de sirga* also gives us a good example of this in the form of the memories of Arquimedes Quintana from the battle of Tetuan. The brutal reality of the experience (which included losing an ear and waking up on a stretcher with the severed head of his general resting on his legs) is softened when he returns because he is able to tell the story in his own way, to willing listeners who regard him as a war hero. Nelson, his apprentice, hears the story so many times that he is able to relive it in his mind as if it had happened to him personally.[26] But it is also Nelson who is equipped to notice the changes that creep into the story over time, especially when Arquimedes gets old and starts to introduce obvious errors into the narration. These kinds of personal memories — and the difficulty of retaining them — are also important in *La galeria de les estàtues*, in which characters are often prompted to remember things when their senses are aroused by familiar smells and sights. These vivid memories are exceptions, however, to the general rule that memories become harder to access over time. For example, Agnès finds it increasingly difficult to remember her husband because 'Les malles del temps es tancaven, els dies teixien tels imperceptibles de cendra sobre el passat, n'enterbolien el record' ('the meshes of time were closing up, the days wove imperceptible membranes of ash over the past, and dimmed the memory of it').[27]

These problems with the way our memory functions become crucial to the operation of creating a sense of group identity, which is something that Moncada explores in detail in *Camí de sirga* and *Estremida memòria*. It is not only individuals who shape the narrative of their own lives through memory and forgetting, but communities too. One good example of this is the opening of *Camí de sirga,* in which we are told that various aspects of the first days of the destruction of the town in 1970 are vividly remembered years later: the clock on the bell-tower stopped working the day before as if as a symbol of what was to come; there was total silence as morning dawned, then the great shock of the noise of the first demolition. The only problem is that all these eye-witness accounts are revealed to be 'absolutament falsos'.[28] In fact, no one except Honorat del Rom actually noticed when the first house was demolished, and the guilt of this realization is what leads people to construct more 'appropriate' memories, given the importance of the event. This does not mean that they are necessarily lying: a combination of the fallibility of memory and wishful thinking is responsible, rather than mendacity. The end result is the creation of a collective memory — or myth — of the day that further unifies the community by signalling the importance of the date for all its members.

One of the similarities between myth and memory is that they both have general frameworks that are relatively stable, but these enclose a level of detail that is changeable and unreliable. One of the reasons why myths such as 'Noah's Ark' or 'Atlantis' have been able to resonate over many centuries is that they are adaptable to new circumstances and can hold similar meanings even for very different cultures. Whether as a biblical tale, a children's book or the basis of a Hollywood film, these are instantly recognizable and require little intellectual effort to appreciate them. (In fact, this is why one critic, Josep Lluró, found *Camí de sirga* unchallenging and criticised the fact that its underlying structure outweighed other more important literary elements.)[29] The details of the mythical story can change but the essential meaning remains, and as psychologists have shown, this is the case with memories too. No matter how badly we might have mixed up individual details, the broad outlines of what we remember are generally correct. For example, the band did play on that occasion in 1931 whether or not it contained a trombone.

This is where the structures of myth and memory coincide with those of history and narrative. When we hear or read a story, either a fictional or historical one, the most important part of our immediate reaction to the story is its general plot and development. Only on the second and subsequent occasions can we also take in a lot of the incidental detail. According to Northrop Frye:

> The continuity of a work of literature exists on different rhythmical levels. In the foreground, every word, every image, even every sound made audibly or inaudibly by the words, is making its tiny contribution to the total movement. But it would take a portentous concentration to attend to such details in direct experience: they belong to the kind of critical study that is dealing with a simultaneous unity. What we are conscious of in direct experience is rather a series of larger groupings, events and scenes that make up what we call the story. In ordinary English the word "plot" means this latter sequence of gross events. For a term that would include the total movement of sounds and images, the word "narrative" seems more natural than "plot" [...] The plot, then, is like the trees and houses that we focus our eyes on through a train window: the narrative is more like the weeds and stones that rush by in the foreground.[30]

Myth, memory and literature therefore have very similar structures, in which details have a secondary importance to the basic plot. So when, for example, in *Estremida memòria* the writer Jesús omits the details of Emília's vist to the gentlemen's club, the important information she gathers there is the main thing the reader needs to know, not the details of how she acquired it. As the errors in Arnau's extended version reveal, details add atmosphere and have an important impact in their own right, but are much more easily interchangeable.

In a work of literature, after the direct experience of the first reading we have the chance to read again in order to absorb more of the narrative detail. In myth, the first 'experience' of the generic plot is lost in time, but we are always able to re-read the plot and re-write the narrative to suit our present needs. In memory, because the events come from our own direct experience, we believe that with anything we vividly remember we are always re-reading the same plot and the same narrative, but this is an illusion. Individual memory becomes collective myth or history only when these imperfect memories are shared. However, the telling of memories brings social pressure to bear on the teller, which lead him or her to distort the story, even if unintentionally. In *Camí de sirga* and *Estremida memòria*, Moncada narrates the processes by which tales are told, distorted, disputed and finally absorbed into the collective consciousness, constantly reminding us that the collective history of the people of Mequinensa is untrue in anything other than its broad outline. Nevertheless, the process is important because it creates a sense of community that allows Mequinensa to stand out as a special collective.

Local, national and global histories

One of the ways that Mequinensa is seen to be special is in its resistance to Francoism, even after the war. This contrasts with the fictional Torrelloba of *La galeria de les estàtues* which instantly embraces the Nationalist cause and remains convinced of the validity of the regime even in the tough times of the 1950s.[31] In the case of the Mequinensans who do join the Nationalists, this is normally not entirely their choice, as in the cases of Bernat and his aide Xapa.[32] The history of Spain during the Civil War and Franco regime is one of the themes that runs through the first two novels, presenting a stinging critique of the hypocrisy of those times.

This critique is achieved especially through the use of irony. Two very good examples of this, with similar structures and effects, are the cases of the missing bridge and the sun rising in the west, to be found in *Camí de sirga* and *La galeria de les estàtues* respectively. The first incident concerns the bridge over the river which had been blown up by the Republicans as they retreated from Mequinensa, meaning that the old ferry had to be brought back into service. The townspeople are astonished to read a press report a few years later that the bridge has been rebuilt when they have seen no evidence of building work: they rush to inspect the site and sure enough the bridge is still in ruins.[33] Nevertheless, a military convoy attempts to cross the fictional bridge, and when they ask directions to it Honorat del Rom is arrested for telling them it does not exist. He is freed not long later when the convoy comes speeding back from the uncrossable river just long enough to pick up the soldier who had been left to guard him. The irony here is developed both through the situation, especially in the bathetic way it is resolved, and character, as the polite and hesitant Honorat is contrasted with the overbearing and confident official.

The very beginning of *La galeria de les estàtues* contains a similarly ironic incident introduced by the memorable line 'A l'ínclita, catòlica i gairebé immortal ciutat de Torrelloba, el sol eixia per l'est' ('In the illustrious, catholic and almost immortal city of Torrelloba, the sun rose in the east').[34] The story concerns the civil governor of the province who was making a speech to honour the placement of a bronze bust of Franco in the town at the end of the Civil War. Comparing Franco several times to the rising sun, he continuously points to the west rather than the east. This disconcerts the people of the city who ask themselves '¿tant havien canviat les coses amb el nou règim? ¿Era possible que els vencedors fossin capaços de capgirar també les lleis astronòmiques?' ('had things really changed so much with the new regime? Was it possible that the victors were even capable of turning the laws of astronomy on their head?'). They are therefore relieved to find that the next day the sun rises in the east just as it had when Spain was a monarchy and then a republic. Similar elements are present here as in the first example: bathos, and the contrast of an over-confident official with a hesitant but pragmatic response from ordinary people.

Another crucial factor in both cases is the skill with which Moncada describes the situation, using language with a high, formal register to show the pomposity of the officials and the absurdity of the situation.

Other ways in which the regime is criticized do not depend on irony but on either direct description of historical events or reference to incidents in the lives of the characters. For example, in *Camí de sirga* two of the important characters die in a Nazi concentration camp having been exiled from Spain, and many minor characters also die as a direct result of the war or its consequences (see for example the brief story of Llorenç de Veriu on pp. 13-4). The senselessness of the conflict is also captured in the paintings with which Aleix de Segarra decorates the walls of the former convent. Originally a design featuring nymphs and goddesses, Aleix externalizes the mental pain caused by the war by painting instead images of dead friends and acquaintances killed by the Nationalists.[35] This is an interesting narrative technique as it gives a sense of the escalation of the conflict through a very immediate visual device as the paintings advance. (A similar technique is used in *Estremida memòria* when Feliu draws on the walls of his cells in order to tell his version of the crime and his part in it.)[36] Moreover, the paintings are then destroyed by the bulldozers as the town is demolished, providing another visual representation of the way the town's memory of these former residents is diminished as the fabric of Mequinensa is destroyed.

The Civil War is not the only war to feature in *Camí de sirga*. I have already mentioned Arquimedes Quintana's memories of the battle of Tetuan, the period of prosperity brought by the First World War, and the way the Second World War touches the townspeople by claiming the lives of some who thought that they had escaped such a fate by fleeing to France. These kinds of historical events obviously have a thematic function, but they also are used more generally as devices to establish the historical and chronological framework for events that are more personal to the characters in the novels. For example, at one point we are told that 'L'expectació al voltant de la nau de la vídua Salleres va amortir fins i tot el ressò de la gran ofensiva alemanya de final de març del 1918' ('Excitement at Senyora Salleres' boat even eclipsed the great German offensive of late March 1918')[37] Statements such as this have several effects, of which providing a time reference is only the most obvious. In this particular case, there is a certain irony in the launching of a boat being perceived as more important than a world war, and this makes it a good example of the way that Moncada uses war as a tool to link the particular and the universal, the microcosm and the macrocosm. The boat is more important to the townspeople because it is closer to home and more tangible, yet the First World War, as a 'universal' event, is more widely recognisable as a marker of historical time, and is still a part of the town's collective experience in its own right.

Historical references to war are also key to *La galeria de les estàtues*, as the action of the novel takes place mainly within two conflicts a couple of decades apart: the Civil War and the war in Ifni. The wastefulness and brutality of both wars are explicitly highlighted by the parallel murders of father (Alexandre) and son (Dalmau) during these conflicts. These kinds of external events are not as obvious in *Estremida memòria*, where events have a simpler chronology and are either set in 1877 in the weeks following the crime, or in 1995 while Jesús is writing his account of it. Even so, history still provides an important backdrop since 1877 was early in the Restoration period and some of the brutality of the treatment of the prisoners and their supporters can implicitly be explained by the uncertainty of the times. (The importance accorded to Genís de Borbó's surname is one indicator of this.) There are also passing references to historical figures such as King Alfonso XII or events like the First World War or Civil War.[38] Most importantly, Garrigues gives a potted history of recent events, including the 'Glorious' Revolution and the rapid return of the monarchy, in his monologue while rowing Agustí Montolí across the river.[39] This means that there is still a strong sense that the story has an identifiable setting within important periods of Spain's real history. All three novels can therefore be said to contain elements related to the genre of the historical novel, and act as a chronicle of the misfortunes of Spain in the nineteenth and twentieth centuries.

One of the most important aspects of this portrayal of Spanish society is its political and class-related divisions. I have already mentioned that in *Camí de sirga* Mequinensa is portrayed as pretty much unanimously Republican, although there are a few pro-Francoists among the upper classes. Senyora Salleres is an interesting character in this respect as she does not conform to the stereotype of her class and instead shows a level of humanity (or maybe pragmatism) that contrasts with the haughtiness of the Torres clan. After the war she is happy to re-employ staunch Republicans such as Nelson, unlike other employers who ostracise anyone who was very politically active on the Republican side.[40] Their attitude only changes once the Second World War brings a new demand for lignite and therefore an new period of prosperity. Desperate for workers, they then abandon their beliefs because of the desire to make money.[41] Torrelloba is portrayed as the opposite of Mequinensan society: it is the middle classes who are dominant and the characters singled out to represent the city in *La galeria de les estàtues* are priests, military men, educators and the governing classes. Their hypocrisy, corruption and greed is similar to that of the employers in Mequinensa but the difference is that in Torrelloba they are in the majority rather than the minority.

The portrayal of Mequinensan society in *Estremida memòria* is interesting and perhaps more nuanced than in the two previous novels. The crime implicates the whole of Mequinensa in one way or another, not just the poorer members of society from which the actual criminals are drawn. Relationships between the different levels are complex and their true extent is often hidden. In some cases they represent an abuse of the poor by the rich, as in the case of Eladi de Torres who lends money to Marta when the family is in a desperate situation and takes possession of her house when she cannot repay him.[42] However, there is also generosity, as when Guillem de Segarra teaches Amàlia to read and write.[43] In fact, Moncada highlights the idea that it is literate people of whatever background who are more likely to question the treatment of the prisoners and the validity of the death sentence.[44] The existence of written accounts of the events alongside the oral histories also highlights the different mechanisms by which we construct such genres.

Genre and Literary Influences

The final section of this chapter will concentrate on the techniques of writing employed by Moncada himself. It has already been pointed out that his works have some elements of historical fiction, since they situate the fictional lives of the characters within a faithful and recognizable historical framework. Moncada himself said that 'pel que fa als fets històrics, procuro reflectir la realitat, mai no falsifico una dada, un fet o un personatge real per interessos de ficció. La ficció va per un altre camí, la diferència és que jo no faig la història d'uns fets, sinó una novel·la on aquests fets tenen un paper; el fet és manté però la trama és una altra.' ('As far as the historical facts are concerned, I try to reflect reality, I never falsify data, facts or real people in the interests of fiction. The fictional aspects are of a different kind, the difference is that I'm not writing a history of a set of facts, but a novel in which these facts have a role to play; the fact is still there but the plot is different').[45] It is the accuracy of the setting that permits the critique of the Franco regime and of certain sections of Spanish society. However, the works are not historical novels per se, or at least not *just* historical novels.

One of the main descriptions that has been applied to Moncada's work is that it belongs to the genre of the rural novel. Around the time of publication of *Camí de sirga* critics identified a tendency among a group of writers to shy away from themes relating to city life and instead look to areas of the Catalan-speaking world outside the metropolitan area of Barcelona (see the introduction to this volume). Moncada himself rejected the label of 'rural novelist' in the same way that he rejected comparisons with magic realism.[46] It is true, however, that a sense of geography is key to the setting and themes of his novels, and that this geography is most noticeable when he is talking about Mequinensa and its surroundings, that is, when it is a semi-rural geography. The movement of people through the streets of Torrelloba that he describes in *La galeria de les estàtues* actually uses a similar technique, but it does not have the same symbolic meaning as descriptions of the streets of Mequinensa in *Camí de sirga*. Sandrine Ribes has spoken about 'a mimetic topography' in Moncada's work, not just in *Camí de sirga* but also in the short stories, since the fictional Mequinensa created by Moncada simulates the real town while not being exactly like it.[47] In the novel, the destruction of each house or street releases the personal memories of those, like Nelson for example, who are witnessing it, and therefore this topography also takes on another kind of mimetic function, symbolizing the pathways of memory and the gradual loss of these pathways as the real objects that act as stimuli for memory are pulled down. The physical destruction of the town also represents the breaking down of historic and current links between members of the community.

Another key element in this symbolic topography is of course the river, and its associated towpath.[48] When these are cut off by the dam this has the same effect on the community as the destruction of the houses, since the river was the life-blood of the community both economically and in terms of its identity. It is no coincidence that the novel ends by describing the fate of the old barge Neptú as it is broken up by the surge that results from a violent rainstorm. Obviously the river can also be regarded as carrying a whole host of other meanings related to time, history and life itself, but these meanings are always intimately connected to the actual town and people of Mequinensa and are not just general philosophical musings. The particular geography of the area is therefore a fundamental part of Moncada's work.

This emphasis on geography and history (along with myth and the collective identity of the people of Mequinensa) suggests that Moncada is more interested in these elements than in the psychology of his individual protagonists, and this is to some extent the case. Only Dalmau of *La galeria de les estàtues* is a completely rounded protagonist whose inner world is consistently explored in detail.[49] In other cases we tend to see snapshots of a character's psychological state, most notably in the case of Carlota de Torres whose anguish during the destruction of the town is used to represent the general feelings of the townspeople. Another example would be the way that the mental states of Aleix de Segarra and Feliu Noguera are represented through their use of art (see above). In general, though, each novel is composed of multiple voices and characters and, apart from in the case of Dalmau, they represent the collectivity of which they are a part rather than pretending to be complete portraits of an individual. This means that even Moncada's sophisticated understanding of the psychology of human memory is revealed more through its operation to create collective memories than through looking into the mind of any one individual.

One final genre that needs to be mentioned is that of crime fiction. While not even *La galeria de les estàtues* could be said to be a typical detective novel, despite the presence in it of policemen and a series of murders, the influence of the crime genre on the plot and structure is clear. In *Estremida memòria* the genre's presence is subverted by the fact that although the novel revolves around a crime the guilty parties are quickly identified and so this is not the principle mystery; nor are the agents of law and order the focus of the plot. However, there remains a mystery to be solved (what part did Feliu and Simó really play in the crime?). Even in *Camí de sirga* the reader is faced at the start with the mystery of why the town is being destroyed, and the full reasons for this are revealed gradually as we learn about the history of Mequinensa. While not being related to crime fiction, as such, the novel still has elements of mystery that help the overall movement of the plot.

Even though the question of genre, especially in terms of the label of 'rural novel', has been an important one for critics of Moncada's work, in the end what is more significant is the skill with which Moncada combined a number of elements and influences. As Northrop Frye has said, any great work of literature 'draws us to a point at which we seem to see an enormous number of converging patterns of significance'.[50] With their detailed explorations of myth, memory, history, storytelling and the particular world of Moncada's fictional Mequinensa, the novels certainly do reveal a large number of such patterns, which seem to fundamentally converge in the exploration of how a group of people successfully constructs and maintains its collective identity.

Notes

[1] Xavier Moret, 'Estremida Memòria de Jesús Moncada', *El País*, 6/10/2005, pp. 1-2.

[2] Ramon Sistac, 'Territori, llengua i identitat en l'obra de Jesús Moncada', *Urc* 21, 2006, 64-8, p. 67. See also Mercè Biosca, 'Aproximació a la llengua i a l'estil de Jesús Moncada', in *Guia De Lectura de Jesús Moncada*, ed. by Emili Bayo and Mercè Biosca (Barcelona: Magrana, 1992).

[3] CdS, p. 36.

[4] Emili Bayo, 'Jesús Moncada: La memòria més enllà de les aigües', in Bayo and Biosca, pp. 7-45, p. 41.

[5] Marta Nadal, 'Jesús Moncada, novel·lar l'absència', in *Vint Escriptors*

Catalans, ed. by Marta Nadal (Barcelona: Publicacions de l'Abadia de Montserrat, 1997), pp. 189-97, p. 193.

[6] Kathryn Crameri, 'The Location of Myth in *Camí De Sirga* by Jesús Moncada', *Journal of Iberian and Latin American Studies*, 8, 2002, 41-54, pp. 43-5; Sandrine Ribes, 'Le Mythe dans *Camí De Sirga* de Jesús Moncada', *Revue d'Études Catalanes*, 2, 1999, 159-81, pp. 169-71.

[7] Crameri, 'Location', p. 44; Ribes, 'Le Mythe', pp. 165-9.

[8] E.g. CdS, pp. 9-14 & 92-4.

[9] CdS, p. 5.

[10] GE, pp. 408-12.

[11] GE, pp. 230-3.

[12] GE, pp. 264-6.

[13] GE, pp. 366.

[14] GE, p. 33.

[15] GE, pp. 415-20.

[16] GE, p. 7.

[17] EM, p. 308.

[18] EM, p. 191.

[19] EM, p. 205.

[20] EM, p. 211.

[21] EM, pp. 232-6.

[22] Jordi Capdevila, 'Jesús Moncada: "Els contes que semblen més fantàstics són els més reals"', *Avui* 22/10/99, 1999.

[23] CdS, pp. 93-4. English translation from *The Towpath* trans. by Judith Willis, p. 67.

[24] EM, p. 70.

[25] CdS, p. 141.

[26] CdS, pp. 35-6

[27] GE, p. 261.

[28] CdS, pp. 9-10.

[29] Josep M. Lluró, 'Tendències de la narrativa catalana dels vuitanta', in *70-80-90: Literatura*, ed. by Àlex Broch et al (Valencia: Edicions 3i4, 1992), 113-39, pp. 132, 134.

[30] Northrop Frye, 'Myth, Fiction and Displacement', in *Literary Criticism and Myth*, ed. by Robert A. Segal (New York & London: Garland, 1996), 119-37, p. 120.

[31] GE, p. 199.

[32] GE, p. 222.

[33] CdS, pp. 281-3.

[34] GE, pp. 7-8.

[35] CdS, pp. 182-3.

[36] EM, pp. 268-70.
[37] CdS, p. 74. English translation from *The Towpath* trans. by Judith Willis, p. 51.
[38] EM, pp. 33, 350.
[39] EM, pp. 67-70.
[40] CdS, p. 220.
[41] CdS, pp. 235-6.
[42] EM, pp. 255-7.
[43] EM, p. 84.
[44] Kathryn Crameri, 'Forging the Community: Explorations of Memory in Two Novels by Jesús Moncada', *Modern Language Review,* 98, 2003, 353-66, p. 364.
[45] Maribel Ollé, 'Jesús Moncada: 'Jo no faig la història d'uns fets, sinó una novel·la", *Avui*, 27 April 2002; see also Sandrine Ribes, 'L'Oeuvre de Jesús Moncada: Quand l'écriture devient mémoire', unpublished PhD thesis, Université Montpellier III — Paul Valéry, 2006, p. 217.
[46] Xavier Moret, *Jesús Moncada*, Retrats 7 (Barcelona: Institució de les Lletres Catalanes, 2005), p. 38.
[47] Ribes, 'L'Oeuvre', pp. 270-8.
[48] Ribes, 'L'Oeuvre', pp. 278-291.
[49] Sandrine Ribes, 'Personatges i autobiografia en l'obra Moncadiana', *Urc* 21, 2006, 117-21, p. 119.
[50] Northrop Frye, *Anatomy of Criticsm: Four Essays* (Princeton N.J.: Princeton University Press, 1957), p. 17.

Extract from Estremida Memòria[1]

Translated by Kathryn Crameri

1

The man spoke in a low voice, 'Dead, Your Honour; more than dead, extremely dead', as if he was afraid of failing to show enough respect for the bodies that he had found and had come to report.

Despite the seriousness of the case, which almost seemed unreal in the suffocating heat of that August afternoon, he had to suppress a laugh as he put aside the paperwork concerning a never-ending case about a farm that was being fought over by a mob of heirs, who were going at it tooth and nail. Standing in front of the table, oblivious to the effect of the deathly superlative, or the clarification 'I'm not the judge, my good man, I'm just the scribe', the nervous peasant poured out in fits and starts the circumstances of his macabre find: at first he had thought they were asleep, 'Even though it was very strange, Your Honour, to decide to take a snooze there in the baking sun', but when he saw the blood, that was already dry and black, and the terrible wounds covered in greedy flies, he had shuddered in horror. He couldn't see the guard properly because he was lying face-down. The other person, a civilian, was on his back, 'I think he's the tax collector, Your Honour', looking at the sky with wide-open eyes.

He stopped the informant, 'Sit down and wait', and sent a constable scurrying off to find the judge. Despite the urgency of the message, the magistrate, who had been caught by surprise in the middle of a most pleasant siesta, took a long time to turn up and did so with bad grace, 'What's going on, Montolí? Why the hurry?', giving off a nauseating smell of sweat mingled with cigar smoke. While Don Silvestre, now that he had grasped the importance of the matter, 'Good God, what a mess! What a bloodbath! Why didn't you tell me earlier Montolí', closely questioned the informant, he put in motion preparations for the court to visit the scene of the crime, 'Les Planetes, Your Honour, near Vallcomuna, on the border of the districts of Casp and Mequinensa'. After much commotion, the expedition finally got under way after six o'clock.

***

It was already midnight before the feeble cries for help reached them from the valley. Their lanterns diverted from the path to concentrate on some bushes, in the middle of which lay badly injured one of the guards that escorted the Bank of Spain's tax collector, who, as had been confirmed by a telegram from Mequinensa, had left the town at dawn on his way to Casp. They had been attacked by bandits at ten o'clock in the morning, he moaned, while Teòfil examined him and administered first aid. His colleague and the tax collector were corpses; he had seen how they had been finished off after they fell down wounded. He had deceived the criminals by playing dead. He had no idea what had happened to the mule driver or the animals that were carrying the money. When the bandits had disappeared, he had got out of the area by dragging himself like a worm. Mad with pain and thirst, he hadn't dared to show any signs of life until he heard friendly voices.

They found the bodies straight away. In the meantime, a detachment of cavalry from the Mequinensa garrison turned up, reinforced by a group of local people, including one of the mule-driver's uncles. They were leading one of the mules, which they had just found on the way, heading back to Mequinensa with empty saddle-bags. Since it would be difficult to carry out a search at night, 'Solomon', as Teòfil called Don Silvestre, ordered that investigations should be suspended until the next day.

He hadn't slept a wink. The wailing of the guard bothered him, but he was even more worried by the thought that the mule-driver might also be badly hurt and they might not arrive in time to save him. The lad's uncle and other Mequinensans, paying no attention to the orders given by Don Silvestre (who had settled down after giving them and was sleeping like a baby), were searching the area by lamplight. The anguished voices, 'Artur, don't be afraid, it's us; Artur, speak to us', followed one another in a fading litany. And even though Teòfil was right to say 'he was either an accomplice of the bandits or he's dead; so he's not going to reply in either case', he wanted to think about the other possibility, which was unfortunately the most unlikely one.

***

'Sir?'

Startled, he realises that he's in the Sailors' Inn in Mequinensa, and not in Vallcomuna on the road to Casp. The little man with the miraculous images[2] is looking at him with concern.

'Are you alright?'

'Yes, yes thanks.'

The landlady comes over to his table.

'Someone's asking for you', she says to him.

'For me?', he says, unable to hide a gesture of surprise.

2

'Thank you, Cinta', says Senyora Eva, giving her back the little case after taking a pill from it, 'put it back in its place so that I've got it handy if I need it in the night'.

The image of the bleeding heart, illuminated by the flame from the nightlight, takes her back to the evening of August 25th as soon as she enters the bedroom: she hears once again the din of the cavalry in the street and the terrible cries of the cook, which seem to be lying in wait to link her, implacably, once more to the thread of memory.

***

She and Severiana had run down the stairs when they heard her. Joana, in shock, could hardly get the news out: something terrible had happened at Les Planetes, near Vallcomuna. There was talk that people had died; maybe it was war again... Her heart — 'Les Planetes you say?' — missed a beat. Artur had gone out at dawn, the tax collector had hired two mules from him to carry the money. She had been frightened when she learned that they would be escorted by two Civil Guards who had come from Maella especially for that purpose. 'Civil Guards? Does that mean that there's some kind of danger?' But Artur had reassured her: routine precautions, 'What do you think is going to happen, woman?'.

They had run out of the house. At the door, she narrowly escaped falling under the wheels of the carriage belonging to her masters, who were coming back from Lleida. Blind to everything, 'Where are you going, Cinta' asked a frightened Senyora Eulàlia, 'What's going on?', she hadn't even turned around. The dust thrown up by the soldiers' horses still hung like a fog in the street, as groups of horrified people made their way down to the Ebro. Cavalry troops and armed townspeople were getting on to the ferry. One of Artur's cousins, in tears, gave her the news that had been received by telegram at the castle: they had found the bodies of the tax-collector and one of the Civil Guards near Vallcomuna. They knew nothing else. The court from Casp was already on its way to the scene of the crime.

***

The flame of the nightlight placed in front of the Virgin of the Bleeding Heart trembles in the draught. It also trembled at midday on 26th August, the day after the events, when she and Senyora Eva, 'Come on, dear, let's pray that nothing has happened to him', received the news as they knelt at the priedieu: they had found Artur that morning. Murdered by gunshots and blows from a sword.

3

Tomorrow it would be three months since she had been to the cemetery or sat by Oscar's grave to tell him all the news from the town, from the house, well, anything that could soothe him in death and offer him any consolation regarding his unchangeably deceased condition. Three months, since the last Sunday in August.

She was restless that day — she remembers it vividly — and couldn't wait for the sun to go down. Even though a boiling hot north wind was lifting up great dust storms around the olive groves and the Segre seemed motionless in a landscape discoloured by sun, she didn't feel the heat. She had astonishing news and couldn't wait to tell Oscar. She paused a moment at the gate of the cemetery to adjust her black headscarf and brush the dust off her skirt: the wind had turned her mourning clothes white. What would he say, a man who was always so refined, fastidious and poised, so fussy, if he saw her in such a filthy state? She slipped through tombstones and crosses without even glancing at the work being carried out on the pantheon that Eladi de Torres was having built on the East side, drawing scorn from Senyor Maties de la Picarda, 'A pantheon? It looks more like a fairground stall. Am I right or not, Eugeni? Am I right or not, dear Filomena?'. In front of the tombstone, 'Marble, Justina', the Administrator had said to her on the day it was erected, 'our masters have spared no expense', the importance of the news meant that she could skip the excuses that she generally felt obliged to present for their son. The lad, 'Oh, that Genís', had not been to visit his father since the day of the burial, implacably widening the gap that had already separated them in life.

She explained to the deceased in great detail what had happened at Vallcomuna, from the confusion generated by the first pieces of news to the confirmation — that had come at most three or four hours ago — of what everyone feared: that they had found the mule-driver's body on the banks of the Ebro. What had happened to Artur, 'Such a young man, Oscar...', was terrible and had badly shaken her; the next day she would go and give her condolences to the family. Genís sensibly suggested, 'You can see that has a good head on his shoulders', that it was not good to go straight away as other people did, more out of nosiness than sympathy, when the poor people had just received such excruciating news. She took her leave from her husband with the promise of telling him the week's news next Sunday. As she left, the wind threaded the tangled sound of the castle's trumpet between the tombs; in the distant reaches of the valley, under the red dusk, it seemed to her — yes, by God, it did seem to her — that the Ebro and the Segre were coming together like bloodstained sickles.

The next day, Genís went to the deceased's house in the mid-afternoon. As she herself was on her way there a while later, she saw a group of Civil Guards disembarking from the ferry. At Artur's house, the sky fell in on her. The horrible end the lad had met, to which murmured commentaries were constantly adding extra wounds and slashes, seemed even more terrible because of the lack of a corpse and the impossibility of being certain of his death through its physical reality. Furthermore, the lack of a coffin was causing unease: there was no point of reference for expressions of sympathy.

On the first floor, where the ladies were, the atmosphere of desperation took hold of her instantly. She imagined herself in the same circumstances as the boy's mother, with Genís the one assassinated by bandits and buried far from the town. Every visit meant opening the wound anew, provoking further laments. Cinta, the fiancée, the poor girl, was sitting next to one of Artur's sisters. From the floor below there came the whiff of tobacco; the fluttering of fans accompanied the muffled sound of people. The arrival of the Segarra ladies provoked murmurs of gratitude. 'We should be thankful that they are so considerate with Cinta', one of the neighbours muttered in her ear, 'not all rich people would do that', and she felt offended. The observation seemed to imply a slur on the Senyors de la Picarda, who never went personally to express their sympathies and always used to send Oscar. 'There are certain places they can't go, Justina, they need to make themselves respected', her husband used to say in justification. He would show up at masses, vigils, birthdays and funerals, dressed up in his master's black clothes that had been inherited by Eugeni for the same purpose. She didn't have time, though, to reply to the busybody. Strange, heated voices came up from the ground floor and soon melted into an uproar. Then a wave of agitation jolted the women and the first cries were heard. Intrigued, 'What's happening?', she slipped as best she could towards the staircase and from there, between the Segarras' hats that lay abandoned on the landing, she looked down. In the entrance hall there was a throng of people from which there stood out tricorn hats, uniforms, rifles... 'They've taken someone', said Senyora Eva, 'Holy Mother of God, what's going on?'. The tricorn hats were heading towards the door, and the staff were moving aside to let them through. They had a prisoner: Genís.

4

She feels it beside her, like a wolf on the prowl. Lying on the bed, she tries to run away from it by emptying her mind.

'Drink this, Octàvia', says Emilia, forcing her to sit up.

Suddenly, the cry breaks out like the crack of a whip applied to her memory. She chokes, pushes aside the cup that is being pressed to her lips, the infusion spills and soaks her front. The scream brings back the light of August 27th; the pieces of the puzzle fit inexorably together.

***

The daylight, which was still intense even though the afternoon was beginning to fade, softened as it met the border of roses on the embroidery. The half-finished flowers on the bedspread, that were continually being put off because of Feliu's illness, were the only breath of fresh air in the heavy atmosphere that lay over the town. That morning — Emilia was saying, also embroidering at her side — the factory was full of speculation about last Saturday's crime, almost everyone attributed it to a band of Carlists. Even though it was more than a year and a half since the end of the war, there were still groups of rebels in the vicinity who practiced banditry. One of the factory girls had gone so far as to announce that, thinking coldly about it, the only bad thing about the whole business was the death of Artur. As for the rest, when all was said and done, the world could be quite happy about the disappearance of a tax-collector and a Civil Guard. One less blood-sucker, one less tyrant, two more thieves gone to their graves. The poor would be glad of it. It was only a pity that the other butcher had come out alive. As for the money — the fortune that had been extracted from the town —, who cared whether it was stolen by one group or another. Wouldn't it still have lined the pockets of undesirable people if, instead of disappearing on the way to Casp, it had arrived in the capital? Where would it have ended up, in whose pockets? Why wasn't it used to build schools, hospitals for the most underprivileged rather than bleeding them dry for their taxes? Some of the rich, like the viper-tongued Eladi de Torres, talked a lot about progress at the club. They put on a good show. But when all was said and done it was best for them that things didn't change. The more ignorant people remained, the more they would profit. A den of thieves. Emilia didn't say who her colleague from the factory was. Not that it mattered, since many of the townspeople must think the same. The worker had got it right, though: the only bad thing, 'Ill-fated young man, poor Cinta', was the death of Artur.

She was interrupted by cries coming from the smithy. Both of them got up at once, horrified by the same thought: Feliu had injured himself. Someone was coming upstairs at a run. Her husband, racked with fear, appeared on the landing. He didn't even see them, 'Feliu, what's the matter?', and continued up the stairs. That was when the Civil Guards invaded the dining room like a flood, 'Upstairs', shouted the one leading the party, 'quick! Don't let him escape onto the roof', they pushed Emilia aside with a brutal shove. She tried to stop them, 'What's going on, why are you after my husband, what are you trying to do to him?', and one of them slugged her with the butt of his rifle.

***

She barely notices that Emilia, 'Your dress is soaking', is trying to dry her front. The memory of the stink of sweat and leather emanating from the guards overpowers the smell of the spilt infusion: they are trampling over her, swearing, 'Get out of the way you cow', and heading up the stairs. She can hear again the noise of boots on the stairs, the blows, the shouts. They drag a bloodied Feliu down the stairs. She will never forget the words, little more than a hoarse moan, 'Our children, Octàvia', that her husband says as they handcuff him before taking him away.

5

To sleep like a baby, like her Uncle Gastó, to stop her memory... It would only be a question of covering her face with the pillow, pushing down hard. Even if her body decided to rebel with a last impulse against her head's desire for annihilation, what resistance would her paralysed limbs be able to offer? It would be quick, as easy as breaking a dry twig, and, liberated at last, she would melt into the darkness, leaving a lifeless shell behind in the bed. But the plea 'Kill me' gets no reply; Barbara, who has been sitting at her side for a while now, doesn't move.

Maybe, though, they don't have to kill her, maybe she is already dead and in Hell, condemned to eternal immobility, to constantly relive what happened in August and to repeat time after time, always in vain, that she didn't know anything about all that madness. She didn't know anything, and it hadn't even upset her: the crime had taken place in another world, not in the one she had lived in ever since Eladi de Torres' manservant had told her that he wanted to see her. The killings, evoked now and again by Barbara's plaintive drone, 'My Lord, my Lord, what savagery', in sincere sympathy for the victims, didn't concern her, it slid off the shell in which she had sealed herself in order to avoid something that could not be altered. It had been useless to ignore Eladi de Torres' summons. The day after they found the body of the mule-driver, 'My Lord, my Lord', repeated Barbara, 'what savagery, to beat his skull open with a sabre', the manservant came back: his master wanted to see her that afternoon, and no excuses.

The interview plunged her into despair. 'I already gave you six months' grace in January, Marta', was Torres' reply to her plea for another postponement of the loan so that she could write to her son in Barcelona and ask him for the money, 'I can't give you any longer. Think about it: if I started to make exceptions it would be the ruin of me.'

As she was leaving the office in despair, she ran into the manservant. He seemed startled and gave her a funny look before entering his master's quarters. She returned home in a daze and sat on the right hand side of the bedroom balcony. She was overcome, unable to face this disaster. In order to pay her taxes last Friday she had already had recourse once again, lying as usual, to Barbara's meagre savings, and she didn't know where to turn. How could she explain to her husband, her daughter, her son-in-law, to Barbara, that Eladi de Torres was about to take possession of their home as payment for a debt they knew nothing about? How could she explain that she had borrowed money for Jordi, in Barcelona, who had asked for it to get himself out of a tight spot, and that the debt, because she had kept putting off payments despite crippling interest and because of repeated demands from her son, had grown to the extent that she had been forced to sign over the deeds of the house as a guarantee, even though it was the only part of her family's inheritance she still had? At that moment, Soledat had appeared reflected in the balcony window. Behind her, white-sailed barges cut through the burnished silver of the Ebro. She had never seen that expression on her daughter's face. Perhaps she had already heard about what had happened with Eladi de Torres.

She would love to rip the scene from her memory. The horrible and tenacious truth emerges from it every time. When her daughter, instead of talking about the debt, told her that they had just arrested Simó, accusing him of being one of the Vallcomuna assassins, she actually felt relieved.

6

What was the world like three months ago? And what was she like? A pitiless wind seems to drag away with it the images from that time; when she looks at herself in the mirror — one of the wedding presents from her Aunt and Uncle in Riba-Roja — she can't find any trace of them. The old Quima no longer exists, she has forever been left behind on the other side of the border that divided her life on 27th August.

That day, the children were at her sister's house. Her sister-in-law, who doted on her nieces and nephews just as much as Jacint, wanted to make up for the days that they had been away. The investigation made Valentí so mad, 'Catching the criminals will be like tipping water into the sea: who knows where they might have ended up', that he had not come home for dinner. She had taken advantage of his absence to get on with cleaning the house, since she had found it, as she expected, untidy and looking like a tip. Afterwards she had lain down, exhausted, for a bit of a nap.

She had just fallen asleep when Brígida woke her up. At first, her sister-in-law's words, 'They've arrested Genís Borbó, he's one of the criminals', seemed unbelievable. Genís Borbó? 'Yes, woman, yes', she insisted, 'Justina's son'. It was all around the town, they had just got hold of him at the mule driver's house, as he was paying his respects to the family. Uproar, scandal. As they took him off he had shouted out his innocence, of course. Justina was on the first floor, with the women, and when she found out what was happening, she had flung herself down the stairs like a madwoman. Neither the guards nor the constables had given any explanation; they had taken their prisoner away with his mother hot on their heels, begging them to let her son go.

He wasn't the only person arrested, there were two more: Feliu Noguera and Simó Juneda. They had found Marta's son at the Salzes café, not half an hour ago. While some of the guards went in through the door on Barca Street, others were watching the one near the docks. Simó's behaviour had given him away: no sooner had he seen the squad enter than he had leapt out of his chair to run away. After a mad chase, they had got him behind the table and stunned him with blows from their rifle butts amid the cries of the café-owner's wife and the breaking of glasses and bottles.

The town square was already full to bursting. Still incredulous, people were talking in low voices, exaggerating the vicissitudes of the arrests. The one person who must have known all about it was Valentí; but nobody came out of the town hall. Now and again they could make out a movement behind the blinds. Suddenly everyone descended into silence. Two guards had appeared at the entrance: in between them, a swollen face belonging to Simó Juneda; they were followed by another pair with Feliu the blacksmith. Then, third in line, they brought out Genís Borbó.

While she observed in horror the sinister retinue that was at that moment turning the corner, 'They must be taking them down to the prison', mused Brígida, 'what a shock, my God', a stunned outcry erupted. At the door of the town hall a fourth detainee had just appeared: Valentí.

Notes

[1] Part III, Chapters 1.1-1.6. First published 1997.
[2] Translator's note: the man had earlier tried to sell him images of saints.

Select Bibliography
Works by Jesús Moncada

First Editions

Històries de la mà esquerra (Barcelona: Gràfiques Diamant [Premi Joan Santamaria de narració 1971]), 1973.

Històries de la mà esquerra i altres narracions (Barcelona: La Magrana, 1981).

El Cafè de la Granota (Barcelona: La Magrana, 1985).

Camí de sirga (Barcelona: La Magrana, 1988).

La galeria de les estàtues (Barcelona: La Magrana, 1992).

Estremida memòria (Barcelona: La Magrana, 1997).

Calaveres atònites (Barcelona: La Magrana, 1999).

Contes (Barcelona: La Magrana, 2001).

Cabòries estivals i altres proses volanderes (Calaceit-Fraga: Quaderns de les Cadolles, 2003).

Most Recent Editions

Històries de la mà esquerra (Barcelona: Edicions 62, 2004).

El Cafè de la Granota (Barcelona: Edicions 62, 2006).

Camí de sirga (Barcelona: Edicions 62, 2004).

La galeria de les estàtues (Barcelona: Edicions 62, 2008).

Estremida memòria (Barcelona: Edicions 62, 2004).

Calaveres atònites (Barcelona: Edicions 62, 2007).

Cabòries estivals (Barcelona: Edicions 62, 2004).

Works Translated by Jesús Moncada

Anon. *Educació secreta* (Barcelona: La Magrana, 1993). (Under the pseudonym Palemó Llamborda.)

Anon. *Una Dama victoriana* (Barcelona: La Magrana, 1995). (Under the pseudonym Gualteri Llumdivina.)

Apollinaire, Guillaume, *Les proeses d'un jove Don Joan* (Barcelona: La Magrana, 1988).

Chimo, *Les paraules de Lila* (Barcelona: La Magrana, 1997). (Under the pseudonym Fídies Pamboli.)

Cortada, Joan, *Llorenç* (Barcelona: Curial, 1987).

Crébillon, Claude, *Retaule dels costums del temps* (Barcelona: La Magrana, 1989). (Under the pseudonym Metodi Cefalònia.)

de Mairobert, Pidansat *Confessió de la senyoreta Safo* (Barcelona: La Magrana, 1992). (Under the pseudonym Petroni Santapau.)

de Saint Amour, Hippolyte *Memòries d'una puça* (Barcelona: La Magrana, 1997). (Under the pseudonym Jeremies Flit.)

Donville, *Disbauxes* (Barcelona: La Magrana, 1996). (Under the pseudonym Pius Pi.)

Du Bourdel, P., *La senyoreta de Mustelle i les seves amigues* (Barcelona: La Magrana, 1988). (Under the pseudonym Benigne Rosselló.)

Dumas, Alexandre, *El comte de Montecristo* (Barcelona: La Magrana, 2002).

Duponchel-Hankey, *L'Escola de les amants* (Barcelona: La Magrana, 1994). (Under the pseudonym Màxim Petit.)

Hardellet, André, *Feixugues, lentes* (Barcelona: La Magrana, 1989). (Under the pseudonym Gedeó Ge.)

Hoffmann, E.T.A. *Sor Monika* (Barcelona: La Magrana, 1992). (From the original French version, under the pseudonym Gaudemi Gelabert.)

Malet, Léo, *Carrer de l'estació, 120* (Barcelona: La Magrana, 1991).

Martin du Gard, Roger, *Confidència africana* (Barcelona: La Magrana, 1995).

Schroeder-Devrient, W., *Memòries d'una cantant alemanya* (Barcelona: La Magrana, 1988). (Under the pseudonym Pitàgoras Fontcalda.)

Verne, Jules, *Els fills del Capità Grant* (Barcelona: La Magrana, 1996).

La volta al món en vuitanta dies (Barcelona: La Magrana, 2000).

L'illa misteriosa (Barcelona: La Magrana, 2001).

Vian, Boris, *Tots els morts tenen la mateixa pell* (Barcelona: La Magrana, 1993).

Vian, Boris, *Mort als lletjos* (Barcelona: La Magrana, 1994). (Under the pseudonym Baldomer Cerdanyola.)

Walter, Osman, *El fiacre* (Barcelona: La Magrana, 1998). (Under the pseudonym Indíbil Tastaboires.)

Monographs/Dossiers on Moncada's Work

Acín, Ramón (ed.), *Jesús Moncada. Su universo literario* (Zaragoza: Ajuntament de Mequinensa-Departament d'Educació, Cultura i Esport del Govern d'Aragó, 2005).

Bayo, Emili and Biosca, Mercè, *Guia de lectura de Jesús Moncada* (Barcelona: La Magrana, 1992).

Frayssinhes Ribes, Sandrine, *L'œuvre de Jesús Moncada: quand l'écriture devient mémoire,* unpublished PhD thesis, 2006, Département d'Études Ibériques et Ibéro-Américaines, Université Montpellier III — Paul Valéry.

Moret, Hèctor, (ed.), *Cròniques del cerç i la garbinada. Recepció i projecció de l'obra de Jesús Moncada,* special edition of *Urc. Revista literària,* 21 (Lleida, 2006).

Moret, Hèctor, 'Estudi preliminar' and 'Propostes de treball i comentaris de text', in *El Cafè de la Granota,* Barcelona: Edicions 62 (Educació 62, 14), 2006, pp. 9-31 and 145-174.

Moret, Xavier, *Jesús Moncada,* Retrats 7 (Barcelona: Associació d'Escriptors en Llengua Catalana, 2005).

Sasot, Màrio, *Guía de lectura de* El Café de la Rana (Zaragoza: Government of Aragón, 1993).

Various Authors, 'Jesús Moncada. Camí del record', *Serra d'Or,* 550 (October 2005), 37-49.

Various Authors, 'Amb Moncada, a Mequinensa', *Serra d'Or,* 590 (February 2009), 20-29.

Articles

Alcover, Carmen, 'El idilio y la ciudad provinciana en *La galeria de les estàtues* de Jesús Moncada', *Rolde. Revista de Cultura Aragonesa*, 91-92 (2000), 52-63.

Alonso, Vicent, 'Jesús Moncada o l'art de contar amb la mà esquerra', *Caplletra*, 22 (1997), 69-80.

Arnscheidt, Gero, 'Jesús Moncada: *Camí de sirga* (1988)', in Pilar Arnau i Segarra, Gero Arnscheidt, Tilbert Dídac Stegmann, Manfred Tietz (eds), *Narrative Neuanfänge. Der Katalanische Roman der Gegenwart. Einzelinterpretationen* (Berlin: Edition Tranvía, 2007), pp. 246-266.

Biosca, Mercè, 'Noms de casa, renoms i zoònims en l'obra de Jesús Moncada', *Butlletí Interior de la Societat d'Onomàstica*, 43 (1991), 269-277.

Biosca, Mercè, 'L'onomàstica en *La galeria de les estàtues*', *Butlletí Interior de la Societat d'Onomàstica*, 65 (1996), 65-78.

Biosca, Mercè, 'Aprendre fraseologia a través de la literatura', *Actes de les Segones Jornades d'Estudi a la Terra Alta* (Calaceit: Patronat Pro-Batea, 1998), 380-392.

Biosca, Mercè and Moret, Hèctor, 'La projecció i la recepció exteriors de l'obra de Jesús Moncada', *Col·loqui Europeu d'Estudis Catalans, I*, (Montpellier: Université Paul-Valéry-Montpellier III/ Association Française des Catalanistes, 2004), 179-194.

Cònsul, Isidor, 'Jesús Moncada, novel·lar el riu de la vida', in *Llegir i escriure. Papers de crítica literària* (Barcelona: La Magrana, 1995), pp. 129-140.

Corretger, Montserrat, 'Algunes observacions sobre la utilització de dos autors cultes -Joan Maragall i Jesús Moncada- fan de la llengua i de la veu popular en les respectives obres *Visions i Cants* (1900) i *Camí de sirga* (1988)', *Homenaje a Joaquín Díaz*, Cambrils: Trujal. *Folklore* 1 (1991), 101-112.

Crameri, Kathryn, 'The Location of Myth in *Camí de sirga* by Jesús Moncada', *Journal of Iberian and Latin American Studies*, 8 (2002), 41-54.

Crameri, Kathryn, 'Forging the community: explorations of memory in two novels by Jesús Moncada', *The Modern Language Review*, 98/2 (2003), 353-366.

Dasca, Maria 'Aproximació a la novel·lística de Jesús Moncada', *Col·loqui Europeu d'Estudis Catalans, II*, (Montpellier: Université Paul-Valéry-Montpellier III/Association Française des Catalanistes, 2004), 127-139.

Gregori Soldevila, Carme, 'Metaficció irònica a *Estremida memòria* de Jesús Moncada', *Caplletra*, 41 (2006), 131-150.

Malé, Jordi, 'Jesús Moncada (1941-2005)', *Estudis Romànics*, 29 (2007), 635-642.

Moret, Hèctor, 'Lèxic de la navegació fluvial en l'obra de Jesús Moncada', *Archivo de Filología Aragonesa*, 52-53 (1996-1997), 179-220.

Moret, Hèctor, 'Onomàstica mequinensana en l'obra de Jesús Moncada', *Ilerda. Humanitats*, 52 (Lleida, 1998), 187-216.

Moret, Hèctor, 'Una aproximación a la obra literaria de Jesús Moncada', *Cuadernos de Estudios Caspolinos*, 24 (1999), 171-187.

Moret, Hèctor, 'Sis notes a partir d'una lectura mequinensana de Jesús Moncada', *Serra d'Or*, 546 (2005), 41-46.

Moret, Xavier, 'Estremida memòria de Jesús Moncada', *El País*, 6 October 2005, Quadern de Cultura, 1-3.

Murgades, Josep, 'Narrativització de formes simples: l'obra de Jesús Moncada', in *Professor Joaquim Molas: Memòria, Escriptura, Història* (Barcelona: Publicacions de la Universitat de Barcelona, 2003), 759-780.

Quintana, Artur, 'La llengua de Jesús Moncada', *Boletín de Estudios Bajoaragoneses*, 4-5 (Alcañiz, 1983), 227-238.

Ribes, Sandrine, 'Noms de bateaux dans l'oeuvre de Jesús Moncada', *Iris* (Université Paul Valéry-Montpellier III, 1997), 239-252.

Ribes, Sandrine, 'Le mythe dans *Camí de sirga* de Jesús Moncada', *Revue d'Études Catalanes*, 2 (Montpellier: Publications de l'Université Paul Valéry, 1999), 159-181.

Ribes, Sandrine, 'L'evolució de la sàtira de la dictadura a l'obra d'en Jesús Moncada', in *Col·loqui Europeu d'Estudis Catalans, II*, (Montpellier: Université Paul-Valéry-Montpellier III / Association Française des Catalanistes, 2004), 229-240.

Ribes, Sandrine, 'L'oeuvre de Jesús Moncada: entre plume et pinceau', *Revue d'Études Catalanes,* 8-9 (Montpellier: Publications de l'Université Paul Valéry, 2006), 201-225.

Ribes, Sandrine, 'Les enjeux esthétiques de l'intertextualité dans l'oeuvre de Jesús Moncada', in *La intertextualitat de la literatura catalana de la postguerra fins avui: Actes del 2on Col·loqui Europeu d'Estudis Catalans (Béziers, 19-21 de febrer del 2006)*. (Paris: Association Française des Catalanistes, 2006),

407-425.

Rodríguez Fischer, Ana, 'Un encisador racó de món: la Mequinensa de Jesús Moncada', *Serra d'Or*, 485 (2000), 40-42.

Sasot, Mário, 'A la recerca de la infància segrestada', in *Així s'escriu a la Franja (Antologia comentada d'autors de l'Aragó catalanòfon)*, (Calaceit: Institut d'Estudis del Baix Cinca, 1995), 103-129.

Škrabec, Simona, '*Camí de sirga* que no es pot recórrer a peu', *Els Marges*, 76 (2005), 105-118.

Škrabec, Simona, 'Entre les convencions i l'originalitat literària', in *XII Seminari sobre la Traducció a Catalunya* (Barcelona: Associació d'Escriptors en Llengua Catalana, 2005), 17-33.

Press Articles and Reviews

Acín, Ramón, 'Memoria imborrable', *El Urogallo* (November 1989), 72.

Acín, Ramón, 'Sirgando la memoria del Ebro', *Heraldo de Aragón*, 28 September 1989, Artes y Letras, 1.

Castillo, David, 'Artesania autèntica', *Avui*, 27 February 1997, Cultura, II.

Cònsul, Isidor, 'Jesús Moncada, narrador consolidat', *Avui*, 15 May 1985, Cultura, 24.

Cònsul, Isidor, 'Camí de sirga, una novel·la esplèndida', *Avui*, 17 April 1988, Cultura, 51.

Cònsul, Isidor, 'Moncada ressegueix un camí enigmàtic amb un complex final', *Avui*, 28 March 1992, Cultura, V.

Cònsul, Isidor, 'Sempre ens quedarà Mequinensa', *Avui*, 27 February 1997, Cultura, I-II.

Giró, Carme, 'L'última novel·la de Jesús Moncada recrea la postguerra en una ciutat de l'Ebre', *Avui*, 13 February 1992, 30.

Isern, Joan Josep, 'Jesús Moncada: la força de la narració', *Avui*, 15 February 1992, Cultura, V.

Isern, Joan Josep, 'Parla Mequinensa', *Avui*, 4 November 1999, Cultura, I-III.

Malé, Jordi, 'Estremida memòria', *Revista de Catalunya*, 121 (1997), 144-147.

Maresma, Assumpció, 'Moncada contraataca', *El Temps*, 24 February 1992, 68-71.

Moret, Xavier, 'Jesús Moncada, de Mequinensa a Torrelloba', *El País*, 13 February 1992, Quadern, 1.

Moret, Xavier, 'Jesús Moncada en Torrelloba', *El País*, 7 August 1993.

Ollé, Manel, 'De la geografia a la història', *El Temps*, 3 September 1992, 91.

Oller, Dolors, 'Vida perdurable', *El País. Quadern*, 24 March 1988, 5.

Sasot, Mario, 'La ciudad innombrable', *Heraldo de Aragón. Artes y Letras*, 29 January 1993.

Sasot, Mario, 'Un mequinenzano escritor de un río y de sus gentes', *Heraldo de Aragón*, 3 December 1991.

Sasot, Mario, 'Un regreso al relato y a Mequinenza', *Heraldo de*

Aragón, 24 September 1999, 55.

Singla, Carles, 'Jesús Moncada recrea la postguerra amb mots amables', *Diari de Barcelona*, 30 January 1992, 33.

Torres, Neus, 'La galeria de les estàtues', *Revista de Catalunya*, 63 (1992), 158-160.

Vidal-Folch, Estanislau, 'Ocupeu una cadira al Cafè de la Granota', *El País. Quadern*, 26 May 1985, 4.

Interviews

Biosca, Mercè, 'Aproximació a l'obra de Jesús Moncada', *Serra d'Or*, 351 (1989), 55-57.

Biosca, Mercè and Cornadó, M. Pau, 'Jesús Moncada. El riu de la memòria', in *Escriptors d'avui. Perfils literaris*, Ajuntament de Lleida, 1992, 48-51.

Bussé, Xènia, 'Treballar amb Pere Calders no era mai avorrit', *Avui*, 1 February 2004, Diumenge, 6-11.

Castro, Antón, 'Sólo soy un contador de historias', *El día de Aragón (Imán)*, 22 October 1989, 12-13.

'En primer plano: Jesús Moncada, escritor', *El Periódico de Aragón. Domingo*, 2 May 1999, 12-13.

Cid, Josep Sebastià, 'Jesús Moncada: la memòria de la vila entre dos rius', *El Món*, 313, 21 April 1988, 44-47.

Gilbert, Trinitat, 'Entrevista a Jesús Moncada', *Descobrir Catalunya*, 75 (2004), 82-89.

Moret, Hèctor, 'Jesús Moncada: de Mequinensa a Torrelloba', *Batecs*, 14 (Fraga, 1994), 4-5.

Moret, Xavier, 'Ser escriptor ha estat sempre la gran passió de la meva vida', *Avui*, 7 April 2002, Diumenge, 4-9.

Loncà, Andreu, 'Entrevista amb J. Moncada', *URC*, 1 (1989), 36-41.

Muñoz, Josep M., 'La memòria d'un món negat', *L'Avenç*, 288 (2004), 49-54.

Nadal, Marta, 'Jesús Moncada: novel·lar l'absència', *Serra d'Or*, 438 (1996), 53-55.

Ripoll, Josep M., 'Del temps i el riu', *Lletra de canvi*, 8 (1988), 36-40.

Vidal, Pau, 'No escric per mequinensans, barcelonins o catalans. Escric', *El País*, 8 December 2001, Quadern, 1-3.

Translations of Moncada's Work

Aragonese
Camín de sirga, Zaragoza: Gara d'Edizions, 2003. Trans. by Chusé Aragüés.

Danish
Træksti [*Camí de sirga*], København: Munksgaard/Rosinante, 1993. Trans. by Marianne Lautrop.

Dutch
Het jaagpag [*Camí de sirga*], Amsterdam: Meulenhoff, 1992. Trans. by Adri Boon.

English
'Dead man's revenge' and 'A barrel of soft soap' ['Revenja per a un difunt' and 'Un barril de sabó moll]', *Catalan Writing*, 10, Barcelona: Institució de les Lletres Catalanes, 1993, pp. 64-71. Trans. by Patricia Mathews.

'Provisional Report of Elies Santapau's Sprint' ['Informe provisional sobre la correguda d'Elies'], *Review of Contemporary Fiction*, 28/1, 2008, pp. 36-9. Trans. by Martha Tennant.

The Towpath [*Camí de sirga*], London: Harvill/HarperCollins, 1994. Trans. by Judith Willis.

French
Les Bateliers de l'Èbre [*Camí de sirga*], Paris: Éditions du Seuil, 1992. Trans. by Bernard Lesfargues.

Frémissante mémoire [*Estremida memòria*], Paris: Gallimard, 2001. Trans. by Mathilde Bensoussan.

Galician
Camiño de sirga, Vigo: Xerais, 1997. Trans. by Xabier Rodríguez Baixeras.

German
'Dringliche Besprechung' ['Debat d'urgència'], *Wespennest*, 101 (La periferia — Literatur aus Spanien), Wien, 1995, pp. 70-74. Trans. by Georg Picher.

Die Versinkende Stadt [*Camí de sirga*], Frankfurt am Main: S. Fischer, 1995. Trans. by Willi Zurbrüggen.

Die Galerie der Statuen [*La galeria de les estàtues*], Frankfurt am Main: S. Fischer, 1997. Trans. by Willi Zurbrüggen.

'Fußball am Fluß' ['Futbol de Ribera'], Friedlein R., Richter B. (ed.) dins *Die Spezialität des Hauses. Neue katalanische Literatur*, München: Babel-Verlag, 1998, pp. 16-22. Trans. by Roger Friedlein.

Hebrew
עין שמאל של תומם דאטודה ['L'ull esquerre de Tomàs d'Atura'], Tel Aviv: *Iton 77 (Literary Monthly)*, 16 (Tel Aviv, 1995), 48-50. Trans. by E. Sariola.

Hungarian
'Galaxis Joe hátborzongató vallomása', ['L'estremida confessió de Joe Galàxia'], *Nagyvilág*, 30/4 (Budapest, 1985), pp. 534-538. Trans. by Zsuzsanna Tomcsányi.

'A partvidék réme', ['La Plaga de la Ribera'], in *A gondviselés szeszélye.* (*Mai katalán elbeszélök*) (=*Coses de la providencia. - Contistes catalans contemporanis-*), Budapest: Íbisz, 1998, pp. 75-79. Trans. by Zsuzsanna Tomcsányi.

A Folyók városa [*Camí de sirga*], Budapest: Íbisz, 2005. Trans. by Krisztina Nemes.

Italian
'Il racconto del veccio tranviere', 'Storia di giorni dispari' and 'Riunione d'urgenza' ['Conte del vell tramviari', 'Història de dies senars' and 'Debat d'Urgència'], in *Trame di letteratura comparata*, anno II, 2 (Cassino, 2001), Dipartimento di Linguistica e Letterature comparate, 51-79. Trans. by Giuseppe Tavani.

Japanese
Hikifunemichi [*Camí de sirga*], Tokyo: Gendaikikakushitsu Publishers, 1999. Trans. by Yoshiko Tazawa and Ko Tazawa.

Polish
'Przed odejściem' ['Preludi de traspàs'], *Czas Kultury*, 2 (Poznań, 1994), p. 24. Trans. by Barbara Łuczak.

'Plaga Ribery', 'Słowa z oliwkowego drzewa', 'Futbol nadrzeczny' and 'Nastepcy' ['La Plaga de la Ribera', 'Paraules des d'un oliver', 'Futbol de ribera' and 'Els delfins'], *Literatura na Świecie*, 5-6 (Warszawa, 2003), 81-97. Trans. by Marta Cedro and Pau Freixa.

'Lewe oko Tomasza d'Atura', 'Pilna debata' and 'Hektorowi to, co Hektorowe!' ['L'ull esquerre de Tomàs d'Atura', 'Debat d'urgència', 'A l'Hèctor el que és de l'Hèctor'], *Czaskultury*, 5-6

(Poznań, 2004), 194-215. Trans. by Witold J. Maciejewski.

Historie z lewej ręki [*Històries de la mà esquerra*], Poznań: Biblioteka Telgte, 2006. Trans. by Witold J. Maciejewski.

Portuguese
Caminho de sirga, Lisboa: Dom Quixote, 1992. Trans. by Artur Guerra.

Romanian
Rîuri care duc în cer [*Camí de sirga*], Bucureşti: Editura Univers, 1997. Trans. by Mianda Cioba.

Russian
Translations of 'Nit d'amor del coix Silveri', 'Riada' and 'Un barril de sabó moll', in *Rasskazy Pisatelei Katalonii* [Stories by Catalan Writers], Moscou: Editorial Ràduga, 1987, pp. 254-267. Trans. by V. Fiodorov.

Serbian
Srušeni grad [*Camí de sirga*], Beograd: Laguna, 2007. Trans. by Igor Marojević

Slovakian
'Vyhnanstvo bez návratu' ['Exili sense retorn', fragment de *Camí de sirga*], *Revue svetovej literatúry*, 4 (Brastilava, abril 1991), pp. 42-46. Trans. by Vladimir Oleríny.

Slovenian
'Pepel spomina' ['Cendra del calendari', fragment of *Camí de sirga*], *Literatura*, 21 (Ljubljana, 1993), pp. 73-77. Trans. by Jerca Kos.

Proti toku [*Camí de sirga*], Ljubljana: Študentska založba, 2004. Trans. by Simona Škrabec.

Spanish
Camino de sirga, Barcelona: Anagrama, 1989. Trans. by Joaquín Jordá.

El Café de la Rana, Zaragoza: Gobierno de Aragón, 1993. Trans. by Celina Alegre.

La galería de las estatuas. Barcelona: Anagrama, 1993. Trans. by Celina Alegre.

Historias de la mano izquierda, Zaragoza: Xordica Editorial, 1996. Trans. by Chusé Raúl Usón.

El Café de la Rana, Zaragoza: Xordica Editorial, 1997. Trans. by Chusé Raúl Usón.

El ojo izquierdo de Tomàs d'Atura y otros cuentos [selection of short stories from previous translations by Celina Alegre and Chusé Raúl Usón], Madrid: Alianza Editorial, 1997.

Memoria estremecida. Barcelona: Anagrama, 1999. Trans. by José Farreras.

Riada [not-for-sale bilingual edition], Barcelona: Llagut, 2000. Trans. by Alberto Clavería Ibáñez.

'El origen de las especies', in *Mar y montaña. Antología de cuentos catalanes contemporáneos*, Barcelona: Lateral ediciones, 2001, pp. 99-106. Trans. by Jordi Carrión. Also published in *Lateral. Revista de Cultura. Antología de cuentos catalanes contemporáneos (Suplemento especial)*, 76 (Barcelona, 2001), 23-25.

'El origen de las especies', *GRANTA en español*, 4 (Barcelona, 2005), 51-58. Trans. by Julio Hurtado.

Calaveras atónitas, Zaragoza: Xordica Editorial, 2005. Trans. by Chusé Raúl Usón.

Cierzo y bochorno [contains the short stories 'Fútbol de ribera' and 'El ojo izquierdo de Tomàs d'Atura' and the epilogue of *Camí de sirga* previously translated by Joaquín Jordá and Chusé Raúl Usón into Spanish and by Chusé Aragüés into Aragonese; and the Spanish translation by Agustín Larrañaga of the story 'Un grabado del siglo XVII'], Zaragoza: Gobierno de Aragón, 2005.

'Un grabado del siglo XVIII', in *Con ojos ajenos. Aragón*, Zaragoza: Gobierno de Aragón, 2006, pp. 111-122. Trans. by Agustín Larrañaga.

Swedish
Dragarstig [*Camí de sirga*], Stockholm: Norstedts Förlag, 1996. Trans. by Sonia Johansson and Kjell A. Johansson.

Vietnamese
Duòng kéo thuyên: trên sông Ebro [*Camí de sirga*], Hà Nôi: Nhà Xuât Bân Van Hoc, 1996. Trans. by Nguyên Dinh Hièn and Do Si.

The Contributors and Translators

Kathryn Crameri is Associate Professor of Spanish Studies at the University of Sydney, Australia. Her research interests include contemporary Catalan literature, the cultural policy of the Autonomous Government of Catalonia since 1980, and Catalan nationalism.

Dr Stewart King is Senior Lecturer in Spanish and Catalan Studies at Monash University, Melbourne, Australia. He has published widely on contemporary Catalan and Spanish literature and has a particular interest in crime fiction.

Hèctor Moret Coso is a Catalan poet and scholar, and was a close friend of the late Jesús Moncada. He teaches Catalan Language and Literature in Barcelona, as well as devoting a substantial amount of time to projects related to the dissemination of Moncada's work.

Dr Sandrine Frayssinhes Ribes is a *Professeur Agrégé* at the Université Paul Valéry-Montpellier III, France. She wrote her Ph.D. thesis on Jesús Moncada and has published numerous articles both on his work and other Catalan writers.

Judith Willis translated Jesús Moncada's *The Towpath* into English for Harvill. Her other translations include *No Pasaran! Photographs and posters of the Spanish Civil War* and the children's book, *The Grey Boy*. She was one of the translators of Joan Fuster's *Dictionary for the Idle* (Five Leaves/Anglo-Catalan Society).